ISBN-13: 978-0615678382
(Phunkhenaton Publishing Co, LLC)

ISBN-10: 0615678386

Printed in the U.S.A. for Worldwide
Distribution

First Printing: 2012

DEDICATED. . .

to appreciation and application of Universal Living-Spirit, Infinite Intelligence and Power.

CONTENTS

FOREWORD

Have you ever wondered what kind of business man Abraham, Moses or Jesus would be? Or have you ever asked yourself, did David or Paul ever have trouble making "ends meet?" Or did Mary and Joseph have any real life, everyday problems like you and I may sometimes have?

Are you willing to consider, with an open mind and a ready heart some practical characteristics, thoughts and habits of ancient achievers? What is true wealth? Can rich people go to heaven?

Studying the Bible, ancient history and modern science for practical application, has revealed to **many people over the Ages of Man**, a marvelous hope, fear and faith in the GOD of our bible. For the first time in their life, many students can balance the old conflicting beliefs with such scriptures as Deut. 8:18-- *"But you shall remember the Lord your God gives you power to get* **wealth**." And, Gen. 13:5, 6-- "And Lot also, who went with Abraham, had flocks, and herds, and tents. And the land was not able to bear them, that they might dwell together: For their substance was great, so that they could not dwell together."

Unless I be misunderstood, allow to me describe my personal definition of Wealth. Wealth to me is: [1] A burning desire for indepth knowlegde and understanding of

GOD as Primary-First Life, the Originating Source of all living things characterized by Infinite Intelligence and Power. See Jer. 9:24 [2] Inner Peace and Balance. See Luke 17:21 [3] Holistic Health and Energy. I believe that all other forms of wealth can be derived from these.

"But seek you first the kingdom of God, and his righteousness; and all these things shall be added unto you."
Matthew 6:33

Undoubtedly, to many of us the bible can appear very confusing and mysterious. The scripture indeed contains many mysteries and symbolic truths designed to hide its power from diabolical minds, ignorance, and greed. Many other great and powerful truths in history were protected in this manner, such as the Egyptian Mystery System.

Therefore, in this small and introductory volume, we will primarily focus on personal achievement from a historical and pragmatic point of view. However, many important seeds of truths are sprinkled throughout the volume for the most serious minded readers. So, remember that your own power of *Thought, Character Force* and *Action* will bring the best possible understanding.

You may read these verses for the importance of plain and clear understanding: Proverbs 8:7-10, Ezek. 3:4-6, Habakkuk 2:2, Duet. 27:8, 2 Corinth. 3:12. Hopefully, this will help some of you who have not yet realized that our scriptures are not only spiritual; but they are mathematical, historical, symbolical, economical and practical.

This book may appear a little bit unorthodox in that I am actively seeking to get you to adopt a positive attitude toward a life time of continuous, open-minded learning, whatsoever form this personal learning may take. Therefore, I will be encouraging you to study not only your bible; but also other specific books which will help you get more pragmatic understanding.

Also, I encourage you to seek several different authors' perspectives about this subject, recognize and use the commonalties, then investigate the contrast. I urge you to read for personal enrichment more than entertainment, for purpose more than pastime. Study for understanding through open minded investigation and questions. Improve the quality of your life and that of someone you know and love, by applying sound *principles, precepts* and *products*.

ACKNOWLEDGMENTS

To the influence and friendship of my mother, Maxine who showed me how and whom to trust.

To my wife and children; to all of my closet family and friends, I will love you always.

To all of my teachers and mentors over the years; you inspiration continues on.

INTRODUCTION

Success in life has been the desire of most
people since our earliest civilizations.
Imagine, if you can, the tremendous amount
of knowledge or "The Wisdom of the Ages,"
that has passed down over the years.
Instructions and instincts passed from
generation to generation, on how to rise above
survival to abundance and success. Yes,
thousands of years of necessity, curiosity and
practical experience have resulted in
invaluable life guidance for you to use-
today☐

The primary purposes of this book are to
promote and illustrate to you, that the keys to
personal achievement are not only ancient;
they are awaiting your immediate use.
Imagine using the same powerful instructions
that *caused* the prosperity of such giants of
antiquity as Kings Solomon, and David,
Pharaohs **Tut**ankhamen, Ankhenaton and
others and Alexander, the Great, Hammurabi
and others.

If these men were living today, how do you
suppose they would define wealth? What was
Solomon's principal form of wealth? Do you
believe that you can appropriate and use it in
your life? Are you willing to practice your
trust and faith in the Bible and its teachings to
help you realize specific dreams and purpose?

Give such questions a chief seat in your
conscious mind as you unfold the light or

knowledge of this book. You see, nearly all outstanding achievement, since our earliest civilizations have employed the same principles and precepts. This astounding realization is tremendous *cause* for hope, gratitude and **action!**

Surely you seen the magnificent treasures found in the tombs of the Pharaohs of ancient Egypt? A small amount of research reveals that for thousands of years these Pharaohs enjoyed wonderful wealth and balance of life. There were many inescapable commonalities between Anicent Egypt and Ancient Israel; which we will share in some length in Section III of this study reference guide.

However, we will not neglect the considerable evidence of the success traits of many leaders from antiquity. For instance, the ruins of ancient Babylon revealed a city of stupendous ingenuity and prosperity to the eyes of archaeologist.

Remember the three wise men of the CHRIST history; they came from this area. Archaeologists have uncovered in the ancient city of Ur, where Abraham originally lived, evidence of abundance and wealth.

Ask yourself these fundamental questions as read further: What understanding, knowledge and actions *caused* the enormous achievement of the age of the Pharaohs? What specific instructions and counsel *caused* Egypt, Ethiopia and Babylonia to thrive for well over two-thousand years, before any other major civilization? How did they accomplish such goals, desires and dreams?

Similarly, what wisdom and power have *caused* Modern Man to play on the moon and dance in the earth's atmosphere? Consider the stupendous contributions of Napoleon Hill, John F. Kennedy, Helen Keller, George W. Carver, Martin L. King and the millions of men and women who have benefited from their inspirations.

Today you have the right and responsibility to unfold your own potential. It does not matter if your aspirations are as extensive as a cure for world hunger and poverty, or as immediate as providing your children with a true education. You can define and achieve your own success.

This book attempts to provide an accurate and practical review of timeless characteristics, habits, and principles of human achievement. It is not a biography of King Solomon or anyone else. That is to say, I am going to focus more on the "Light, rather than the Lamp."

What specifically did King Solomon teach about achievement and how can you use it in everyday? Now is the time for you to use these instructions to achieve your dreams and help you to constructively deal with adversities.

My emphasis on knowledge and instruction [Light], rather than a person [Lamp] will help you to be more self-reliant and self-confident.

The **Light** *of the lamps, is ancient and forever,*

it has guided the Spirits of ages, since the beginning of time.

*The **Lamp** is like the firefly, who comes only for a season; yet a little while and he shall not be found, he is privileged to carry the flame, only to the seed of a new generation.*

Your success is dependent on your ability to first help yourself, then others. Therefore, I will primarily promote the practical use of achievement principles from biblical and modern times. My intention is to help you derive more practical benefit from your Bible and your study of history.

Similarly, I am encouraging you to invest both time and money in the maintenance of a **PAL**, "**Personal Achievement Library.**" You will build and use your PAL to improve any aspect of your Life that you choose. I will be recommending specific books and tapes throughout this volume for you to include in your **PAL**. Personal growth and development that is based on universal values and principles can contribute more to society than all the churches, schools and governments combined.

You see, after growing up in the intercity housing projects of Montgomery Alabama; I realized that poverty and want are awful task masters. I have experienced the desperation and violence *caused* by ignorance, arrogance and waste.

Most recently, we have all witnessed further degeneration of the ideals of human character as increased racial hatred, substance and sex abuse, unwise exploitation of people and natural resources, institutionalized deceit and cosmetic corruption in every corner of the planet.

Consequently, I would like to emphasize Cause and Effect, which *operates on the Spiritual, **Mental** and Physical planes of reality.* Remember, if we do not or cannot identify and act on the causes of achievement and failure; then we will be subject to the will of others and the winds of chance.

Therefore, **it is very important that you understand and consider practical**, the natural laws and principles that affect human behavior and thinking. This will help you to make full use of the Jewels of Solomon's wealth.

So, Section one provides a review and introduction to the underlying power and knowledge necessary to learn and apply Section II. Section III is a brief review of some of the most powerful precepts and principles found in acient Egypt and correlated with acient wisdom proverbs and psalms. Section IV, is a supplemental for your contemplation and inspiration. Use it to help build the emotional energy you need to persist in your journey to achievement.

My personal request of you is to diligently study this book and follow through on the instructions it contains. It is a reference guide to encourage you to start or continue to improve your **PAL for every member of your family**. Share your insights with your immediate loved ones; teach them so that you may learn more deeply. Personalize your learning so that they are most comfortable to you. Adopt a long distance attitude, to sustain your improvement efforts in spite of distractions or difficulties over time.

With that, it is with the utmost pleasure, which I hope to contribute a little light to the heart and mind of you the reader of the Jewels of SOLOMON'S WEALTH and PHARAOH'S True TREASURES.

SECTION
I

*"And God said; Let us make man in our
image, after our likeness"*
GENESIS 1:26

Which of your loved ones can you afford
not to ask . . .

hat *resources*, *tools* and **opportunities** were you conceived and born with? If the seed of a single acorn can give rise to entire forest; then what is your **potential**? Are you living your possibilities? What are you **accomplishing**?

What **means** of *achievement* do all human beings enter life with, whatever their gender, education, culture or ethnic background? What **Forces** of life contain the seeds of enduring wealth and opportunity?

These questions merit our most profound and personal consideration. You will need some pragmatic answers to the questions above to make full use of the keys to Solomon's wealth. Men and women have used these and related questions to help shape their destinies for thousands of years.

"The thing that *has been*, it is that which *shall be*; and that which *is done* is that which *shall be* done: **and there is no new thing under the sun.**"
King Solomon: Ecc. 1:9

Recognize, with sincere gratitude, that you were literally born with *everything* that you need to begin your personal achievement; such as, the capacity to think and believe the power of choice and reason, knowledge, personal energy and action. Ponder these as inalienable gifts of universal natural origin. Even the most amateur naturalist knows that nature always provides its species with the physical form, instincts and environment necessary to perpetuate itself. Human beings are not the least of these species.

Jesus, when instructing his disciplines, taught them to- "Behold the fowls of the air; for they sow not, neither do they reap, nor gather into barns, yet your heavenly Father feeds them. Are you not much better than they?"

Section one is focused on three categories of natural tools that are available to you immediately. Foremost is your mind-body combination. Particularly, that is your **Mind was born with your Body**, to create and carry out goals, aspirations and plans harmonious with the direction of Universal-Life Force.

As living Minds, men and women have shown that the essence of our being is greater than our physical body. For instance, some individuals with physical limitations have inspired and proven to us that the only real limitations to human achievement are of the mind and heart. Such achievers as President Franklin D. Roosevelt, who successfully resided over the United States from a wheel chair, has consistently displayed this fact. Consider Stevie Wonder or Ray Charles who have delighted many hearts with their songs.

Secondly, such cosmic forces as **Time and Habit** interact with our Minds to *cause* success or ensure your failure, depending on our attitudes and approaches. Our interset is in the practical impacts of these forces on the *execution* of your achievement plans. This focus will help you better use both these powers of nature to win your goals.

Thirdly, cooperation with **universal natural laws of human activity** and conduct is to your success, as oxygen is to your survival. Just as there are immutable laws of physics and chemistry governing the physical universe; there are also *immutable natural laws* which determine the consequences of human thought and interactions. You should, at least be as aware of these natural laws as you are of the force of gravity and the perception of time.

Mind-To-Body:
Your Personal Power Connection

"**Universal Living-Mind** is available to all individual men"- Jahbril Solomoses

"This I recall to my **mind**; therefore I have hope"- Lam. 3:21

ongratulations, you own the most complex *biological computer system* ever known! Suspended in a circulating fluid medium inside your skull is a mass of tissue about the size of a grapefruit, which is intricately connected to an awesome network of over 100,000 miles of nerve fibers.

Mental processes arise from complex electrochemical signals, distributed over a network of neurons (nerve cells) and back. Thus, allowing you and me to consciously think, memorize, calculate, plan and unconsciously oxygenate and circulate blood, regulate glands and other important automatic functions of our beings.

Yes, there is no other creature on earth so perfectly designed for both great and small achievement. Modern researchers point out that the ***design*** *of your entire body* reflects the preeminent role of your brain in coordinating and controlling your body's functions. And, your brain and nervous system are intimately involved with the functions of your mind. These facts illuminate an inescapable law of nature which declares that-- **Form follows Function.**

Solomon's Wealth – Pharaoh's Treasures

That is, everything in nature has *specific design purpose* and instincts necessary to master its particular environment. For instance, the design of birds of prey is aerodynamic, with sharp beaks and claws to catch their food by flight. Also, trees have roots that anchor them against storms and absorb minerals from the soil. They have leaves and branches that grow outward and upward to seek sunlight.

Natural forces mold these designs over time to reflect ever changing environmental conditions and evolutionary perfection. Scientific and historical evidence shows the refinement process in humans from earliest forms until today. Such researchers as Dr. Richard Leaky, an archeologist, Jane Goodall, a specialist in primate studies, and Charles Darwin provided insights into physical and mental development.

Our brain and minds have developed, through the process of evolution, into tremendous tools for achievement. Humankind created great civilizations, scientific achievements, works of art and music. Consequently, men and women have devoted many life times to understanding our intricate structure and inner processes.

☥ Not Mind *or* Matter, but Mind *and* Matter

Dr. Richard Restak, author of "The Mind," shows that research proves an intricate, complex Mind-Brain relationship; which features distributed processing involving the nervous system. For instance, when certain portions of the brain are removed or damaged; corresponding mental processes like memory and language are affected.

You see your brain-nervous system is a highly sophisticated, organic; computer network and the functions of your mental processes are the software. Learn to maintain and use your own **"Personal Computer"** both effectively and efficiently by learning and practicing mental and physical health skills.

Consider your brain, in fact your entire body, as your primary physical tool or **"Organic *personal production* machine"** to help you produce your desired outputs, hopes, dreams and goals. Like any other machine your body absolutely requires fuel or energy and maintenance to operate.

Therefore, take personal advantage of the health and energy products the available Vitamin and Health Food Companies. These companies provide proven "maintenance"; which when combined with adequate rest, exercise and good nutrition can dramatically increase the quality of your life!

All achievement requires some degree of physical action and physical action requires energy or fuel and maintenance. The topic of personal energy is covered in more detail in Chapter Nine.

Meanwhile, consider this excerpt from the book "Brain Power" by Dr. Albrecht my personal inducement for you to include it in your **PAL.** Also, use this excerpt as

Solomon's Wealth – Pharaoh's Treasures

motivation to improve your physical and
mental conditioning now.

**"The analogy between the brain and a
muscle, in terms of the benefits of
exercising both of them, applies
surprisingly well. The evidence we have
compiled so far indicates that you can
improve virtually any aspect of your
brain's functioning by using it, using it and
using it some more. Many people limit their
thinking by assuming that thinking skills
are somehow genetically fixed and simply
failing to challenge themselves. In precisely
the same sense that your heart, lungs, and
muscles improve their functioning after a
few weeks of jogging and continue to
improve with a steadily increasing exercise
program, your brain skills improve over
time if you make steadily increasing
demands on them."**

Obviously, the amount of energy and exercise
you need depends on your current physical
and mental conditioning. For instance, if your
occupation is pouring and working concrete
foundations, you need enough physical energy
(electrolytes, glucose, etc.) to do the job.
Conversely, if you are a politician, you
probably use more mental energy. Remember,
however that everyone needs adequate
physical exercise, nutrition and rest, whatever
their occupation.

Given the intricate relationship between your
mind and body, including your brain and
nervous system, what is the relationship
between your thoughts, physical activities,
and personal circumstances? According to Dr.
Napoleon Hill's research, the physical

Mind-Body

condition of men and women is largely
decided by the nature of their dominate
thoughts.

Dr. Hill observed and documented that people
who experience poverty, and lack, think about
it more than they think about prosperity and
abundance. Conversely, people who dominate
their conscious awareness with thoughts of
abundance and success are more likely to
experience it.

This research points out two extremely
important points for you to grasp and use.
First, you tend to do or follow-through on that
which you think about most. So, when you
consciously keep your mind on the things that
you want, you are more likely to do those
things which cause them to occur in your life.
*"You will keep him in perfect peace, **whose
mind is stayed on you**, because he trusts in
you."*
Isaiah 26:3

To illustrate, strategically place pictures,
poems and any other visual reminders of your
wants, needs or desires in your home and
work place. Put them in obvious places like
your kitchen or bedroom and near the door
ways that you use most. Carefully select
music, television and friends which constantly
encourage you to do the things necessary to
cause your desires and aspirations.

Secondly, your mind will compel you toward
the object of your dominate thoughts. To
understand this, you should recognize that
your mind consists of two primary functions.
The first of these functions, the **Conscious** or

Solomon's Wealth – Pharaoh's Treasures

Objective mind, is responsible for reasoning, choice and other thinking skills. For instance, you are consciously choosing to use this book.

The other function is the *Subconscious;* that is it operates below your conscious awareness. Your subconscious mind is the largest and most powerful function of the two. It controls all of your essential involuntary processes like blood circulation and oxygenation, breathing, digestion and metabolism. Its two distinguishing characteristics are: 1) It is the builder of the body, and 2) it does not separate reality and imagination.

Similarly, your brain is divided into two distinct sections, the left cerebral hemisphere and the right cerebral hemisphere. The left hemisphere corresponds to the objective or conscious mind. It is characterized by rational, analytical thinking. And, the right hemisphere corresponds to the subjective or subconscious mind. It is characterized by emotional and creative functions, intuition and certain other subjective skills.

Researchers like Jose' Silva and Dr. Karl Pribram, point out that most of the world's educational institutions produce left brain oriented approaches, while neglecting right brain skills. And, no doubt humankind has made enormous advances based on objective-analytical approaches.

However, these approaches have also beset us with overwhelming personal and global challenges. Such as, violence, starvation, pollution, racial and cultural prejudice, national lies, corruptions, deep hatreds and deceits. These physical and mental "land mines" are unavoidable, considering the fact that we have been "going through life with one mind virtually tied behind our backs."

Therefore, the only realistic approach is to learn to use both functions of your mind to achieve specific goals and desires. Again, I offer you an inducement to add "The Power of your Subconscious Mind" by Dr. Joseph Murphy to your PAL:
"Substantial progress in any field of endeavor is impossible in the absence of a working basis which is universal in its application. You can become skilled in the operation of your subconscious mind. You can practice its powers with a *certainty of results in exact proportion to your knowledge of* its principles and to your application of them for definite, specific *purposes and goals* you wish to achieve."

A working knowledge of the interaction of the conscious and subconscious functions of mind is invaluable to your achievement efforts. As mentioned above, a major characteristic of the subconscious mind is that it is amenable to suggestion.

That is, your *subconscious mind can be and is often programmed*. Unlike conscious awareness, your subconscious cannot distinguish between reality and imagination. For instance, a mind under hypnosis will accept as real the suggestion that he or she is a chicken; and proceed to act as a chicken! Professional hypnosis is not a "stage trick," but the application of undeniable mental laws.

Solomon's Wealth – Pharaoh's Treasures

Consequently, any emotionalized thought that persist in your *conscious-awareness*, is conveyed to your subconscious mind by repetition and the *force of habit*. Then your subconscious automates and magnetizes your conscious *attention-awareness* to related thoughts, ideas, people and circumstances.

This process is both definite and certain; however, it's not used consciously enough by most people. Dr. Murphy: *"The habitual thinking of your conscious mind establishes deep grooves in your subconscious mind. This is very favorable for you if your habitual thoughts are harmonious, peaceful, and constructive. "*

These grooves, **which have corresponding physical connections in the brain and nervous system**, produce habitual patterns of thought and action; exactly like grooves on a record album produce sound. Imagine your chances of success if you can consciously impress those grooves, *which cause success and blessing*, into your brain and nervous system!

You can impress upon your subconscious mind, positive thoughts of your own choice, via the principle of autosuggestion or self-suggestion. Autosuggestion is the repetition of vivid images and specific, emotionally compelling desires and expectations to yourself routinely. This repetition of vivid, sensory-rich thoughts and expectations will consequently dominate your conscious, thus calling the *god-like* powers of your subconscious mind into action.

Mind-Body

Autosuggestion is much more effective when you use words, thoughts and commands which are *personally* emotional. You may ask yourself what songs or movie scenes trigger the specific emotions and thoughts in you that you want and need to experience most. Use images and recordings of these to program your own autosuggestions.

A personal example of a simple, yet powerful autosuggestion that I use is: "**Every day and in every way, I AM living my purpose and making it happen.**" When you are practicing autosuggestions go to a place where you are most relaxed, preferably just before you go to sleep at night and right after you awaken. Your subconscious is most amenable when your conscious awareness is most relaxed or off guard.

Develop your own autosuggestions, besides the ones that you will find in the works of Dr. Hill, Dr. Murphy and others. Also, I really enjoyed the mental conditioning exercises in **Sybervision® System's** *Neuropsychology of Achievement* and **Jose` Silva's** *The Silva Method*. Consciously enlist your subconscious to help you achieve your major goals.

In summary, ancient ideas, knowledge and beliefs concerning the mind, heart, body and soul are constantly being updated and unfolded. Fortunately, this has increased recognition of physical and mental human design as a primary achievement tool.

Therefore, remember to express gratitude to your Creator, *Universal Living-Spirit* and *Mind*, for providing you with a mind and body, by developing and using them as best you can. Also, if you do not yet recognize and understand your power, remember to: **"Ask and it shall be given you; seek, and you shall find; knock and it shall be opened unto you."**[Matt. 7:7]

Mind-Body

There is no other creature on earth so perfectly designed for both great and small achievements.

Our mind-brain is an intimately connected unit for a purpose; therefore accept and use this "Personal Computer" to win your desires and needs.

You tend to do or follow-through on that which you think about most. So, when you consciously **keep your mind** on the things that you want, you will be most likely to do those things which cause them to occur in your life.

The subconscious section of your mind will **compel you toward the object** of your dominate conscious thoughts.

You can conclude that systematic, deliberate use of your complete mind (conscious and subconscious) and body is your natural birthright. Express gratitude through your actions.

Time, Habits and Goals

Invisible _causes,_ visible _effects_

"I returned, and saw under the sun, that the race is not to the swift, nor the battle the strong; neither yet bread to the wise, nor yet riches to men of understanding, nor yet favor to men of skill; but **time** and **chance** happens to them all"- wrote King Solomon[ECC. 9:11].

D o you own a watch? Is there a clock in your car or in your home? Do you own a calendar or personal organizer? How often, in a given day do you hear the term Time? The word TIME appears in more than 700 instances in the KJV of the Bible.

Also, you can find several excellent books on managing or saving time. Webster's definition of time occupies one half of a page in the dictionary. Why is time so important that you must reference it so often? Can you see, touch, smell, hear or taste it? No, you can only detect the obvious evidence of its existence.

In fact, there are three known cosmic forces that are _invisible_ in their essential natures, but are _provably visible_ in their effects or results. For the time being, our discussion does not include **GOD Force or that Universal Spirit which moved upon the face of the Waters**; which is the _underlying **Principle of Unity**_ in all elements and forces. I hope to cover this principle in more detail in a later volume.

16

Time, Habits and Goals

Since GOD Force is absolute Unity, the Self-Evident ONE; then this must be LAW in itself. Therefore, all natural laws, whether cosmic, mental, chemical, physical, or spiritual, are but variations or degrees of expression of GOD Force. Thus, a discerning Mind will readily recognize the immediate need to harmonize with certain of these laws.

Cosmic forces of nature are invisible in substance, yet visible in effect. Three of these are Gravity, **Time** and **Habit Force**. I am certain that we don't need to proceed far beyond mention of gravity. Since, Isaac Newton has contributed great insights that have lead to very broad recognition of it.

Instead, for our immediate purpose, let us use gravity as our reference point or evidence that real, yet invisible forces impact our lives constantly. Thereby, opening the way for our acknowledgment of the impact of the *substance* of Time on our achievement efforts.

☥ How do you $pend your time? ☥

Time is obviously, just as real as gravity. It has dominated the conscious-awareness of men and women since our earliest civilizations. For instance, ancient Egyptian stone drawings convey anticipation for the seasons for plowing, planting and gathering of food.

"To *every thing there is* **a season, and a** *time* **to every** *purpose* **under the heaven"** - King Solomon, Ecc. 3:1

Solomon's Wealth – Pharaoh's Treasures

Also, the aging or maturing of all living things testifies of the certainty of the existence of this awesome force. "The glory of young men is their strength, the beauty of old men is the gray head," wrote King Solomon in Proverbs 20:29

Time is an undeniable, element of life. For instance, if you want your dream car within the next ninety days; but do not have the money or the credit, you must know exactly what it will take to get that car within ninety days. You need a feasible and accurate plan of when you are going to do *what*. In particular, a plan is an outline or pattern of events over a specific period.

There are two main reasons for a practical appreciation of time: The first is that time is a ruthless, unforgiving opponent. That is, indecision when decision is required, inaction when action is required, ignorance when knowledge is required will undoubtedly leave you with "***Dreams Deferred***."

Observe the physical or environmental conditions of several people you know. Which of them appear prosperous and happy? Which of them appear frustrated and stalled on the road to personal achievement? How do you imagine each of these people use their time? Which will you model?

The second reason is that you can *employ* time to do anything within your power; through focus and consistency. *Are you willing to direct the power of your thoughts and energy into your specific desires, needs and purpose?*

Time, Habits and Goals

Time is a major key to success at everything from growing plants to winning Olympic gold. That is, when a gardener or farmer plants good seeds in the ground, in the proper season (time), they reap the fruit of their labor at the appointed time.

There are several training classes and books available on the subject of Time Management; such as *Seven Habits of Highly Effective People* by Stephen Covey. If you have not already done so, include some of them in your **PAL**. Practice, patient and persistence develop the muscles, skills and habits necessary for success over time.

What are your major physical and mental habits?

The Force of Habit is closely related to the force of time. Its effect can definitely be felt and seen. What comes to your mind when you hear the terms *compulsion, urge, addiction, pattern and habit?*

Thoughts of needles, allies, gambling casinos, pills and bags may come rushing into your conscious awareness, depending on your background. On the other hand, you may think about practice, patience, or hobbies. What makes all of us feel the definite urge to continue what we consciously or carelessly repeat often? The eternal Force of Habit is the definite major cause.

Habit Force is undoubtedly, the least known of the three major universal forces that I have mentioned to you. Yet, the force of habit is just as profound in its effects on you, as either

Solomon's Wealth – Pharaoh's Treasures

Time or Gravity. Dr. Napoleon Hill's, *Science of Success*, is a good source of information on the practical use of Habit force.

Dr. Hill observed the universal, omnipresent Force of Habit to balance everything in nature through a law of patterns, instincts and habits. Nature observation reveals these instincts and unique patterns of behavior or growth. Why do some birds fly south for the winter, while other ones do not? Why does the sun always rise in east and set in west?

Recognize that there is a certain consistency to anything that is repeated often, including your own thoughts and actions. Learn to use the force of habit to your favor. Otherwise, the Law of Actuality dictates that Habit Force will use you!

Such tragedies as habitual violence, overeating, drug and sex addiction adequately sound this warning. Therefore, always remember that your personal habits and situational reflexes cause success or failure. You'll begin to learn how to develop positive habits of your own choosing in section two.

In preparation for this, you need a practical appreciation of the use of Time and Habit force in achieving your dreams. You see, if you are willing, you can develop all of the habits and reflexes which built Egypt's pyramids, founded the United States and placed humankind in space.

Setting and Achieving Goals . . .

Time, Habits and Goals

is the essence of this chapter. Most of us at one time or another has wanted something specific; made necessary plans to get it, then went and got it! This may have been some thing small like that first bicycle or something major like a college education or choosing a spouse. The point being you set a goal and followed it through.

Mastering your use of time and developing proven habits which cause achievement is a sure way of enjoying the reality of your dreams. However, you must first be specific about what you want or feel that you need. There can be no success if you do not know what you want.

Every self-help book or tape that you may purchase for your **PAL** establishes this truth. Fortunately, if you are not sure about what you specifically want out of this life in exchange for something of equivalent value, there are many resources available to help you. Generally, the self-improvement industry has developed a significant collection of tools and techniques. You will read more about this in chapter five,

-Specific Desire and Purpose-

After you know what you specifically want (your goal), you must _take_ the amount of time, money or other resources you need to accomplish it. It might be necessary for you to devote most if not all of your time and money into your plan to realize your desire. You'll want to consider chapter seven, Prudence and Discretion before you make many major decisions.

Furthermore, if you decide that you have adequate resources to accomplish your goal, you must map out the exact sequence of steps necessary to reach that particular desire or goal. It is very important that your map or plan is accurate and feasible. That is, when you do all of the steps which your plan requires, will they result in the attainment of your goal?

One of the simplest and yet most powerful methods of achieving your goals is to practice what I call "Linear" or sequential planning. That is starting right now from where you are today, decide the most logical sequence of steps that you can identify which will lead you to your goal the fastest.

This method is based on the premise that the shortest distance between two points is one and only one straight line. Fortunately, in practical reality there is always more than one way to reach your goal. However, for your initial planning I advocate linear or sequential thinking; yet you must anticipate flexible execution.

For instance, one of my goals in college was to become a successful computer professional for a Fortune 500 company. To accomplish this goal, I planned to excel in the required business and technical courses; Intern in my chosen field of study. Graduate with honors, and finally interview with such a company to secure my goal within four years.

However, though I secured such a job, it took five years, four jobs and a whole bunch of

Time, Habits and Goals

help from close friends and family to reach my goal. The point is that the plan was accurate and sound, but I had to adapt my execution or action to reality.

You must have or develop the habits necessary to follow through on your plans and adjust them when necessary. You see, Time, Habit Force, your Mind and Body, are stupendous gifts. However, they carry two very sharp edges. Strive to master and use these natural tools to create sound achievement plans and follow these plans to the end.

Cultivate the **Habit of Completion** and **Diligence**, to finish everything that you start. Insist on nothing less from yourself than your full potential. And give thanks and credit to the source of all life, ideas and energy, **Infinite Power and Knowledge.**

Keys Points to remember

There are three known forces in the universe, not including the **GOD Force**, which are invisible in their nature, but provably visible in their effects or results.

Time is obviously, just as real as gravity. In spite of the lack of Newtonian scale research, time has dominated the conscious awareness of men and women since our earliest civilizations.

There are two main reasons for a practical appreciation of time: The first is that time is a ruthless, unforgiving opponent. The second major reason to understand time is that you can use it to do "anything that you want to do."

Habit Force is undoubtedly, the least known of the three major forces of the universe that I have mentioned to you. Yet, the force of habit is just as profound in its effects on you, as Time or Gravity.

Universal Natural Laws and Principles

"She opens her mouth with wisdom, and in her tongue is the law of kindness."
  -King Solomon [Pro. 31:26]

Whenever you watch a Space shuttle launch, use prescription medicine or even pay for your groceries, you are observing the use of the laws of physics, chemistry and mathematics. Appreciate the amount of time, such men as Isaac Newton, Lewis Latimer and Thomas Edison devoted to understanding these laws for our pragmatic use. Today, you can just simply turn on the lights, adding machine, car or computer.

Furthermore, appreciate such ancient scientists and engineers as Imhotep, an Egyptian who contributed significantly to the foundations of scientific application. Imhotep was the Pharaoh's Vizier; which is the same job that Joseph of your bible held when he lived in ancient Egypt. According to Lionel Casson, author of "Ancient Egypt":

"The techniques that produced Egypt's monumental civilization were pioneered by Imhotep, who was Vizier to the powerful King Djoser. At Sakkarah, using small stone blocks instead of traditional, mud bricks, Imhotep constructed for Djoser a step-sided pyramid and a rectangular funerary temple. Nothing like these buildings had ever been seen before."

Solomon's Wealth – Pharaoh's Treasures

You are hopefully familiar with a few of these laws. For example Newton's third law of motion states that for every action (or force) there is an equal and opposite reaction (or force). Similarly, Mathematical laws prove the shortest distance between two points is one and only one straight line.

Webster's dictionary defines natural laws as: A sequence of events in nature or in human activities occurring with unvarying uniformity under the same conditions. We should pay close attention to the phrase "human activities occurring with unvarying uniformity," because it contains a powerful dose of reality.

You see, the primary attribute of all universal natural laws, including mental laws that pertain to human activity, is that they are constant, under the same conditions. For instance, the Sun is at the center of the solar system with all the planets of the system orbiting it in a particular pattern. Therefore, relative to the earth, it always rises in the east and sets in the west.

Your ability to use mental laws depends on intelligent practice and your capacity to believe! The Law of Belief operates on the basis of "the substance of things hoped for, the evidence of things unseen."[Heb. 11:1] This scripture is the biblical definition of the term faith. You see faith is based on hope and evidence, not on blind ignorance and gullibility.

Notice how carefully the author of the book "Hebrews," points out the terms substance and evidence. You can believe that the invisible substance of the laws of physics, mathematics, gravity, time and habit does exist; because you can perceive the evidence of their effects or results.

The evidence of the law of belief is prevalent in the Bible. The terms believe and faith occurs over 474 times, throughout the King James Version. Remember, the standard KJV does not contain all the books of the Hebrew history. You will learn more about belief, in chapter 4.

Your powerful subconscious mind cannot discern fact from fiction; therefore, you must consciously guard against self-limiting beliefs and inaccurate presumptions. It is programmed by the words, images, attitudes and emotions that you allow to dominate your conscious thoughts.

Therefore, strive to believe with sincerity and understanding, things that are based on evidence and patterns of cause and effect. Do this understanding that reality is both visible, like this book and invisible, like gravity or time.

Always exercise an open mind and a discerning heart. Though the law of belief is a considerable asset to invest in your achievement, you also need to understand the relationship between cause and effect.

"For every action there is an equal and opposite reaction"-- Isaac Newton realized. What is your perception of how this law of physics, effects you and your life? Every thing that you do or think is ultimately an action or a reaction. It is either a cause or an effect.

The Law of Cause and Effect is perhaps the most practical of the natural laws. It is not only a foundation principle of this book, but it is also a cornerstone of the Total Quality movement in many economies and businesses. In fact "Cause and Effect" diagrams are techniques which Total Quality businesses use to identify the root or true reason for certain outcomes.

A Cause and Effect diagram is a graphical and methodical way to diagnose a specific problem. That is to establish, with a high degree of certainty, the reason a particular event, action or result occurred. For information you may consult any weel equipped modern library.

Practice observing the conditions and circumstances of your life. Seek the personal cause and cures of your undesirable conditions. Also, investigate the causes of your own or a role model's positive circumstance, to appreciate and keep these.

Practical and creative use of this law promotes steady growth toward the object of any major purpose. Everyone can use this natural law to cause their desires to occur in their life and prevent self imposed limitations. As, you seek to cause the effects in your life that you choose, remember that your thoughts and character will attract people and circumstances to you according to the nature of those thoughts and characteristics.

Universal Natural Laws

Everything in nature attracts and primarily interacts with its own kind. Bald Eagles tend toward other bald eagles, just as Lions live with other lions. Humankind, by the same principle, tends toward places and people that are most like them in thought and action. This is the Law of Attraction.

You are a mental electromagnet, attracting to you the reality of your primary thoughts. Take notice, of your close friends and family members. What do you do when you are together? What do you talk about most? What do you have most in common? Do you enjoy and mutually benefit each other?

Remember you are learning to apply the working principles of natural laws; mental laws that are just as real as the laws of physics. Enlightened Minds applied these principles for over 4000 years as prayers, songs and meditations. People like the ancient Hebrew, King David.

"I will meditate also of all your work, and talk of your doings," wrote King David in Psalms 77:12. Also, he wrote, "I will meditate in your precepts, and have respect unto your ways." Observe David's practice of autosuggestion when you read Psalms 119 in your Bible. You will uncover the master key to his success as a father and a king.

However, recognize with great personal benefit when you study David's life the truth in the cliche "What goes around comes, around." After an incredible mistake of greed and lust, David had Uriah killed, to marry his wife BathSheba, and experienced great personal grief. The mental law that gives this expression credence is the LAW of COMPENSATION.

Much knowledge of the law of compensation passed through such minds as the Ancient Egyptian, Hermes Trismegistus down through such attuned minds as Emerson. Emerson very skillfully unfolds the undeniable power and balance, polarity and compensation in nature. Every thing in nature has an opposite and counterbalance that appears to make it whole; such as, male and female, upper and lower, in and out.

Napoleon Hill very actively promoted and advocated Emerson's essay on Compensation. Do not miss the wisdom in Dr. Hill's direction. Emerson very beautifully described the operation of the Law of Compensation, Polarity, Habit Force and Cause and Effect.

The law of compensation is one of the working principles behind The Golden Rule, "And as you would that men should do to you, do you also to them." [Luke 6:31] Jesus further explained- "It is more blessed to give than to receive." These scriptures are not only beautiful verses to live by, they testify of the messiah's excellent understanding and use of the law of compensation.

Every act has its compensation, whether it is mental or physical. Therefore, strive to treat everyone you meet with mutual respect, understanding, equity and justice. Learn to listen for understanding, question for clarity and speak tactfully to inform. This will help you to recognize yet another variation of compensation known as the LAW of POLARITY and The Complement of Opposites.

Have you ever wondered why it appears that "opposites attract" rather than similarities, as described in the law of attraction? What is the nature of apparent opposites and by which principles are you affected by this law?

Consider these opposites: spirit and matter; man and woman; subjective and objective; in and out; upper and lower; yes and no. Although many of these opposites are contradictory, like fire and ice or motion and rest, there are some opposites that more clearly complement each other.

This is a very important perspective of the polarity of nature. Unfortunately, this undeniable paradigm can and has been used for any purpose. He, who has ears to hear, let him hear. He, who has eyes to see, let him see.

What appears to be mutually exclusive, that which cannot occupy the same space and time, is often exact complements for this very same reason. You see there is a time to every purpose and a role for everything in nature, including human nature.

The apparent extremes of polarity and all the degrees between are often used to serve a given purpose more fully. For instance, the states of deep sleep and full consciousness are apparent opposites. Yet, for purposes of good health and achievement you must have and use them both.

Solomon's Wealth – Pharaoh's Treasures

Similarly, nature has evolved nocturnal
animals to hunt at night; While others are
diurnal or active exclusively in the daylight.
By that, nature fulfills the whole purpose of
survival and perpetuation of species.

This complement of opposites appears in the
"opposite sex" of gender differences
throughout nature. For instance, the anatomy
of male and female is designed to unite them
into one form like a puzzle.

Very often in nature, both form and behavior
may appear opposite to a surface observation.
However, closer examination reveals that each
extreme complements the other in order to
achieve a common purpose. For example, a
dominant male lion is maned and usually does
not hunt for himself. While the lioness does
not have a mane and maintains the dominate
role in the provision of food.

Similarly, in many bird species the males are
bright in color, while the female is the exact
opposite, usually a brown or grayish brown.
This strategy helps to ensure survival and self-
continuity.

You should be able to better recognize this
law of polarity and its effects on the behavior
of men and women toward one another. It is
an undeniable aspect of natural law. However,
in people this law is most useful when
appreciating the true diversity of gender.

Remember- Form follows Function- in
everything of nature, including humankind.
Specifically, males and females are designed
to balance and complement one another. Try

to remember this when you are relating to those of the opposite gender.

Practice mutual understanding, respect, patience, and sensitivity when dealing with anyone who appears very different. You see practice makes positive use of the LAW of USE.

The essence of this law is- "Use it or Lose it." Dr. Edward Deming, the father of the Total Quality management, advocated this principle as: Continuous improvement of products and services, Constancy of purpose, vigorous education, training and retraining. These principles work for both organizations and individuals.

Practice and persistence are the virtues of application or use. This is one of evolution's greatest secrets of "natural selection" and "survival of the fittest." Those muscles, habits and skills that are not exercised or reinforced will decline by this immutable law of nature.

Even the most amateur athletes, know that fitness is achieved and sustained through effort. Exercise all of your major muscle skills, particularly your brain! Use your "Personal" computer as often as you can with full hope and expectation.

HOPE is truly a noble principle and value. It is a sister of Faith, which is a trusting belief based on substance and evidence. Hope is like an oasis to a desert traveler who is crossing the burning sands of life and the oceans of time. Hope is the inspiration of a high school dropout, who is also a single parent and a drug addict. Hope in the object and purpose of biblical faith is life.

Hope is the expectation of a particular desire, need or want. "For there is hope of a tree, if it be down, that it sprout again, and that the tender branch of it will not cease."- Job 14:7 Many people have experienced or seen this principle robs the grave, insanity ward and prison of their victims. Through hope we persist by overcoming desperation, discouragement and hopelessness.

You see, when we human beings are desperate, discouraged and feel hopeless we tend toward our most basic natures or worst. If your basic abilities to cloth, shelter, feed or protect yourself and our loved ones have ever been seriously jeopardized, you understand the value of hope.

Wars, Seditions, Murders and Thievery all testify of the results of human hopelessness. The principle of hope helps to soothe these ravages to body and mind. "Let he that stole steal no more: but rather let him labor, working with his hands the thing which is good, that he may have to give to him that needs"- wrote Paul to the Ephesians [Eph. 4:28]

I ask you, who are wealthier, a destitute person who has hope in GOD, or a person materially rich who finds no reason to trust, respect or hope in anything? Similarly, if you are significantly over your desired weight, savor the sweet taste of the hope of your regaining your desired condition, as you take action to improve.

Universal Natural Laws

Share this natural gift with someone who needs a little boost or who needs a reason to persist. "But sanctify the Lord God in your hearts: and be ready always to give an answer to every man that asks you a reason of the hope that is in you with meekness and fear"-- 1 Peter 3:15. Whenever I have felt the need for encouragement, support and personal action I welcomed the uplifting influences of hope. Share with others that hope and trust which you would have shared with you.

TRUST is the corner stone of any serious relationship; whether it's personal or professional. This ancient imperative is stamped on the U.S. coins and currency as "In GOD we trust." The founders of this country were both wise and correct to establish this reminder on our money. This should help us to keep money in its proper perspective, as means or a tool. "Blessed is the man that trust in the Lord, and whose hope the Lord is." [Jeremiah 14:8]

Trust is the assured reliance on the character, ability, strength or truth in someone who is trustworthy. Trustworthiness means that there is reason to trust someone or something. Like hope, trust is truly a wonderful form of wealth to share with someone who needs it.

This principle has guided the successful decisions and action of many achievers since antiquity. Read the Book of Psalms to appreciate this point. Your family and friends should trust you; therefore, you must remain trustworthy. Similarly, if you are in business, you must be able to trust your business partners. Your customers trust that you will give them your best possible value at a good price.

If you're like most people you've experienced a major breech of trust at one time or another in life. To this I say, always maintain your own standards, values and principles with an open mind and without condition. To be trusted, remain trustworthy. And when this is not reciprocated or appreciated, move on toward your chosen destiny. The laws of compensation, attraction and the Golden Rule will continue to operate.

The GOLDEN RULE:

"Do umto others, as you would others do unto you"

Who on the planet or in heaven does not want to be treated with respect, dignity, equity, integrity and justice? The Golden Rule is truly a universal principle which combines the virtues and values of human ethics. If everyone living would simply learn how to and "do unto others, as you would have others do unto you" we would automatically eradicate many problems.

My observation of the international business community is that it's rapidly learning to assimilate this ancient ideal into practical business strategies. The powerful and effective principles of Total Quality embrace an operating philosophy of "Customer Satisfaction"; which is to give you and me the best possible products and services at the best value or price.

Innovative and forward thinking companies are treating the consumers the way they themselves, as consumers would like to be treated when they purchase products and services. This is the essence of the Golden Rule.

Dr. Napoleon Hill showed his personal reverence for this principle in starting his national publication "Hill's Golden Rule magazine" and subsequently in all his books and lectures. In the "Law of Success," Dr. Hill accurately accredits such giants of antiquity as Jesus, Plato, Socrates, and Confucius. Also, Dr. Hill accredits modern achievers like William James and Ralph Waldo Emerson for his personal understanding of the universal natural law directly behind this principle.

This Law of Correspondence is truly universal, immutable and powerful. It means that our external conditions largely correspond to the nature of our internal condition-"As above, so below; as below, so above" or "As within, so without; as without, so within."

Again, the ancient wisdom of Hermes Trismegistus stands the test of time. He taught the secret of this principle of correspondence thousands of years ago to students who were sufficiently prepared and attuned to receive it. Buy and study The Kybalion published by The Yogi Publication Society, Masonic Temple, and Chicago, IL.

Keys Points to remember

☥   Universal, Natural Laws govern the environment around us; operate upon and within all Living things.

☥   Universal Natural Laws and Principels declare themselves and are axiomatic truths.

☥   Use the referenced titles and other materials to learn more for your practical and spiritual benefit.

In Summary,

You were born with natural tools, resources and opportunities to accomplish your definite desires and needs. If you are living your potential, you are living the proof of this stupendous fact. You are enjoying your accomplishments; the fruit of your labor.

Stop, and think a moment about the amount of knowledge, on survival and achievement, gathered, recorded and organized since 6000 B.C. It fills several buildings in many places around the world; including churches, libraries, foundations, government buildings, schools, and studios. Furthermore, it exists in life's experiences, nature, music and oral traditions.

Out of these enormous archives of history and science, modern scribes are making the use of this information more concrete and practical. Our approach is to illuminate or light up the patterns of "**Cause and Achievement™**" that reach all the way back from our earliest civilizations, up through today and beyond.

You are now aware that your Mind and Body are incredible gifts of Primary-First Life. "Life provides for itself in the living." Your brain and nervous system in particular, housing certain functions of the mind, is your most "Personal" Computer. Practice and exercise of the Mind develops skill, competence and results. Your Mind is your most precious asset, protect and use it wisely. ***Purposely*** develop and use your **PAL** to help you ***awaken*** the enormous, inalienable power at the center of your being. "A word to the wise is sufficient."

You are also aware that your Habits and use of Time, largely decide your success or failure. You know now that these two *invisible forces* will **visibly** *shape your destiny by* **chance**, *if you fail to shape your destiny* **by choice.** Understand this truth far better than you understand the effects of gravity, because it is more useful to your achievement.

You also, are more aware of the effects of universal natural laws on the human experience. Natural laws which govern the consequences of your every thought and act. Diligently ponder and meditate on them to develop your skill at using them. That you may enjoy enduring riches and wealth. **With that, let's make it happen; let's do it!**

SECTION
II

"So God created man in his own   image, in the image of God created he him; male and female created he them."
Genesis 1:27

sk yourself expectantly: How can I use the enormous powers available to me to achieve my specific goals and purpose? What **principles** did King Solomon live his life by? And, how can I profit from them today? What **habits** or teachings guided the behavior and thoughts of Solomon's father, King David? And, how can I use them today? What specific **knowledge, understanding**, **habits** and **characteristics** did Jesus share with Abraham, Daniel, Moses and the ancient Egyptians Hermes Trismegistus and Ptah-Hotep?

What do the Presidents of the United States have in common with the Pharaoh's of ancient Egypt? What habits and principles do men and women of modern achievement, share with the ancients?

The real value of accurate history is not in the knowledge; rather, it is the application of the knowledge to specific goals, opportunities and purpose. The universal natural wealth, described in section I, was not alien to our ancestors. Their understanding of the invisible forces of life, speak clearly from the time worn ruins of their age.

Their accomplishments speak for themselves, testifying of the pioneering and use of sound principles of successful living. This section focuses on those precepts taught and lived by the ancient Egyptians, Hebrews and Greeks. And, adapted, clarified and demonstrated by such outstanding minds as Emerson, William

James, Napoleon Hill and Martin Luther King Jr.

Plan to reread this section again, after you have read the entire book. Adopt and adapt Benjamin Franklin's approach to building these principles into your character. That is, plan to understand and assimilate or get one set of principles at a time, until you have succeeded in building your success habits and reflexes to order.

Obviously, the value of these biblical principles in harnessing natural and eternal forces is tremendous. Therefore, my testimony is that the Bible is the number one "Self-development" literature on the planet.

Exercise the power of your free-will to choose and decide right now to take control of yourself and make a positive difference in your immediate environment. This is the main purpose of this section; to replace chance and "trial and error" with choice and purpose.

Study, this section with all the practical expectations of your achievement efforts. Practice its instructions often and discuss them with your loved ones. Plan to teach a minimum of three people in your immediate life to learn and use the principles of this section. These three people should be yourself and one person from within your family, another outside your immediate family. Teach each other and support one another through the tough spots. "Make a positive difference, make it happen now!"

"Hear this, all you peoples;
give ear, all you inhabitants of
the world, low and high, rich
and poor together. My mouth
shall *speak* of **wisdom**, and the
meditation of my heart shall be
of **understanding**. I will
incline mine ear to a parable; I
will open my dark saying upon
the harp."
Psalms 49:1-4

WISDOM and FAITH

"Buy the truth, and sell it not; also *wisdom*, and   *instruction*, and *understanding*."
   -King Solomon

isdom and Faith are undeniably two of the most prominent principles in your Bible; each principle occurs 234 and 247 times respectively. This is more than any of the other biblical principles that you will use to win your goals. How can you get and use biblical principles of achievement? By using mentors (wise, loyal advisors) and role models.

It is a well known fact that role models and (or) mentors are one of the best means available to learn successful strategies for achieving goals. Notice, that every practical system of instruction examines successful people! Modern self-improvement literatures abound with celebrity testimonials and consolidate first hand experiences of contemporary achievers. Fortunately, historians and archeologist add valuable dimensions or insights for us to combine and contrast the modern with the ancient.

No two characters in history are more readily associated with the qualities of Wisdom and Faith than King Solomon and the most famous

Nazarene, Jesus. Therefore, let's examine more closely their use of these essential principles.

Wisdom is the quality of being wise; sound judgment based on knowledge, discretion or a penetrating intelligence. The patterns established from the context of its use emphasize a deep spiritual quality of understanding and knowledge. This principle first appears in the book of Exodus and extends in use through the book of Revelation. Wisdom is learned through instruction and experience [JOB 12:12, 13], or obtained directly from GOD [Psa. 111:10].

As you can see, knowledge and understanding are significant aspects of the principle of wisdom. Therefore **learning** or the process of getting knowledge, skill or understanding by study, instruction or experience, is crucial to the attainment of wisdom.

Recall that from birth until you reached adequate maturity and responsibility, someone else was responsible to teach you. Our minds are at the mercy of our teachers, including parents, instructors, preachers and counselors for a significant portion of our lives.

As a result, many do not know how to teach themselves from personal initiative, because they did not *learn **how** to learn* or *choose*. Instead, many of them **only** learn what *to choose* and *learn*. Therefore, they do not take advantage of the fact that learning is a life-time process. Dr. Einstein is quoted as having said "The more I learn, the more I realize how much I do not know; the more I realize that I do not know, the more I want to learn."

Consider it very wise to continue your education in an area of your own interest and choice. Whether you decide to do it in a public or private school, church, library, safari or on the streets of America's homeless; learn to love learning.

Develop specialized knowledge in any area that you truly love and proceed immediately to share those skills to help others improve their quality of life. Apply the Law of Compensation and the Golden Rule on this point, and you will experience yet another universal natural law called the **Law of Increasing Returns**.

Recall from section I, the principle of your subconscious mind as an electromagnet, attracting to you the reality of your dominating thoughts and emotions. Observe Solomon's use of ancient autosuggestion in getting the object of his renown. Consider this underlying analogy: 1) The seed of **Definite Desire** is planted deep in the heart's mind using **trust** and **belief**. 2) The fertile soil of **Infinite** Power and Intelligence receives the seed and provides the harvest. 3) Harvest is gathered and used for **Definite Purpose** and responsibility.

☥ Definite Desire is planted deep in the Mind

Notice that Solomon would not have desired wisdom, were it not for the influence of his father King David. "*Only the Lord gives you wisdom and understanding*" David instructed him. [1 Chron. 22:12]

This points out for you the crucial value of instruction and the personal quality of being instructable or teachable. The author has personally experimented with the quality of being teachable by striving to practice the Golden Rule and cultivating a pleasant personality.

I have found that "instructability" causes success! That is, you may get the wisdom of many years of practical, first hand experience simply by seeking out and following sound **instruction**. Accurate instruction saves many years of trial and error in discovering and using that which is readily available. To develop this quality, follow the habit of visibly expressing to your "Instructor," gratitude and appreciation. Use their instruction when possible.

Dr. Hill made this point very simply in organizing the world's first practical system of personal achievement. Again, if you have not already done so purchase and use his works immediately! In the book *The Law of Success*, he amply describes the value of a pleasant, sincere personality, personal tolerance or patience with others.

Furthermore, consider with great personal benefit PROVERBS 4:1-7:

"Hear, you children, the *instruction* of a father, and   attend to know *understanding*; for I give you good doctrine; forsake you not my law. For I was my father's son tender and only beloved of my mother. *He* taught me also and said to me, let your heart retain my words; keep my commandments and live. *Get **wisdom**, get **understanding***; forget it not, neither decline from the words of my mouth. Forsake her not and she shall preserve you; **love her** and she shall keep you. Wisdom is the principal thing; therefore, get wisdom; and with all your getting, get understanding."

There are two points in these verses that I would ask you to **do**. They are as follows:

1) Literally, take the instruction that David offered to Solomon; learn to love wisdom and instruction. Wisdom and instruction, like knowledge and understanding, are very powerful achievement aides when applied to specific goals and purpose. Study *The Master Mind* by Theron Dumont to learn to purposefully cultivate this *association* of the eternal **emotion** of **love** with learning and principle based instruction.

2) Seek to understand the instructions. Asking yourself relevant questions offers perhaps the best bridge to understanding. Ask these questions of yourself for genuine understanding, fully expecting to get appropriate answers. Do I recognize the natural laws or principle at work? Where can I get more information? What value does this have to me; how can I use it?

"Take fast hold of instruction; let her not go. Keep her; for she is your life."
Proverbs 4:13.

Solomon's Wealth – Pharaoh's Treasures

Reflect on the discourse that Solomon relates to you of his parenting from David, that understanding and a burning desire (love her) for wisdom is significant. David had apparently proven to himself, through persistent use of Faith, the importance of deepness of desire for wisdom. Read Psalm 119 in your bible.

Recall that he followed the habit of silent meditation at least three times a day and constantly held his attention on the things for which he prayed! You can immediately see a strong cause and effect relationship between this personal success habit, applied wisdom and faith and David's successful reign as King of Ancient Israel.

So that you might not easily pass over this point, ponder the personal value of David's sincerity in his prayers and in his parenting. What were his personal rewards in return for his sincerity? What universal natural laws are set in motion by our every thought and act? Can you recognize the use of the principle of autosuggestion on the subconscious mind or "the heart's mind" in his techniques?

If you will take the time right now to understand and use David's example you will not need to study the remainder of this section! However, finish studying it for comprehension preparation.

So can you see that Solomon became a wise King, by first being a wise son? That is by accepting his father David's counsel to sincerely seek wisdom.

WISDOM and FAITH

Notice that the quality of being wise is identified with several other characters in the bible, both before and after King Solomon. For instance, we learned from ACTS 7:21-22 "When he was cast out, Pharaoh's daughter took him up and nourished him as her own son. And Moses was *learned in all* the **wisdom** of the **Egyptians**, and was mighty in *words* and in *deeds*."

The ancient Egyptians and the Babylonians were very learned and renowned for their science. You are invited to pursue detailed review of these historical facts in the works of Gerald Massey and others.

For more recent evidence, George Washington Carver exercised considerable knowledge in unlocking the secrets of the peanut and other scientific pursuits. Through wisdom, knowledge and faith, Ghandi and Dr. Martin L. King organized truly significant movements in their respective lives. Dr. Napoleon Hill through wisdom and faith organized the world's first practical system of economic self-improvement.

Also, study carefully the emphasis of wisdom and knowledge or the lack of it, in the book of Job. Wisdom is obviously a prominent principle in the conversations between Job and his fellows. It occurs twenty-three times directly, following knowledge which occurs thirteen times.

Read and reread Job Chapter 28, when sincerely searching for practical motivation and instruction. Ask yourself expectantly -- How can I use this knowledge for my personal

mission and life purposes? The amount of
time you'll spend studying JOB will pay vast
dividends of true wealth in wisdom,
understanding and faith.

**Living-Mind receives the seed and provides
harvest**

Second, Solomon presented his deep desire
for wisdom to Infinite Intelligence or
Universal Living-Mind; who responded in
greater proportion than the desire! This is the
Law of Increasing Returns. Wisdom from
YAHWEH, through sincere prayer and action,
comes in greater degrees of intensity and
amount.
Observe: "Be**cause** you have *asked* this thing
and have *not asked* long life; neither have
asked riches for yourself, nor has asked the
life of your enemies, but has asked for
yourself understanding to discern justice;
Behold, I have done according to your words:
Look, I have given you a **wise** and an
understanding heart, so that there was none
like you before you, neither after you shall
any arise like unto you. And *I have also given
you that for which you have not asked*, both
riches and **honor**, so that there shall not be
any among the Kings like you all your days.
And *if* you will walk in my ways, to keep my
statutes and my commandments, *as your
father David,* then I will lengthen your days.
And Solomon *awoke, and behold, it was a
dream*"[1 Kings 3:10-15]

In recalling the principle of your subconscious
mind you learned that the best time to offer
your autosuggestion is just before going to
bed and just after awakening. Notice the

verse in ***bold italic*** for the evidence of the effectiveness of this practice.

Harvest is gathered and used for Definite Purpose

Third, Solomon learned more about wisdom and understanding by personal experience and by teaching. It is a well known fact that teaching anything that you have learned is a very good way of learning it more deeply.

The entire books of Proverbs and Ecclesiastes are sincere, practical, principle based instruction and precepts. The purpose of these books is for our use in living our lives and obtaining worthy goals which harmonize with universal laws and principles. Reread Proverbs 1:1-6 to understand this stupendous truth.

Solomon applied his wisdom to everything that he could fulfill the original purpose of his desire. You may recall that his purpose was to fulfill his duty to GOD, Family, and Country.

Ecclesiastes 2:12-13 reads- "And I (Solomon) turned myself to behold wisdom, and madness and folly; for what can the man do that comes after the King? Even that which has been already done. Then I saw that wisdom excels folly, as far as light excels darkness."

****

Please study and consider carefully the seeds of Solomon's troubles later in life. These two verses plainly magnify the tragedy of misapplying powerful truths. However, if you will please allow me a diversion for the sake

of my feeling toward this role model. I will show you more about the dangers of the human mind. You see the truth is that our subconscious minds are magnets; attracting the dominate influences that we thoughtfully or carelessly present to it, and then transforms them into realistic experience. Your "heart's mind" cannot discern between good and bad, which is the conscious mind's responsibility through will power. Whether it is for "experimentation" or definite desire if you have any doubts about a choice being good for you and yours or not; remember King Solomon's life in his old age! Reread 1 Kings Chapter 11.
****

You can see plainly now some ways to practice getting and using this biblical success principle. You've now considered three major points concerning Wisdom, namely-- That wisdom is to be sincerely desired; Wisdom is gotten through experience, instruction and Infinite Intelligence; and finally that Wisdom should be applied to our most noble, worthy and definite purposes.

☥Are your beliefs preventing your achievements? ☥

To have a more complete hold of the true value of this principle we must link our examination of wisdom to the principle of faith. I believe, based on my own experience and from study of the experiences of others; that wisdom cannot be perfected without applying the essential quality of faith.

Therefore, let's again use our best role model of the complement of these two principles. Jesus, according to Josephus, a Hebrew historian who lived during Jesus's day, was wise and full of faith.

Faith is beyond doubt the hallmark of achievement of our most perfect role model in biblical history. The entire history of his life on earth is a study in the cultivation and perfection of the wisdom of faith applied to human experience. Therefore, to make practical use of our faith we again need a practical definition.

"Faith," according to Hebrew's 11:1 "is the *substance* of things hoped for, the *evidence* of things not seen." Think about the highlighted words in the biblical definition of this working principle. The substance or object of your hopes, desires and needs is your primary reason for prayer, belief and action.

Is the substance of your hope tangible or intangible; is it visible or invisible? If the object of your goal is either intangible or in the future you must expect and believe that you will obtain it before you can put your faith to use!

A relevant example of an intangible goal to acquire is WISDOM, UNDERSTANDING and FAITH. "How much better it is to get **wisdom** than gold! And to get **understanding** is rather to be chosen than silver." instructs Solomon [Pro. 16:16]. These qualities are very worthy desires; Yet you cannot see, smell, touch, taste or hear them. However, you can detect the evidence of them spiritually and intellectually!

These examples illustrate that it is prudent to have some reasonable evidence on which to base your belief, trust and faith. Nature observation (Psalms 19:1) and the Bible provides limitless evidence of God as Infinite Intelligence and Power, Universal Living-Mind.

Therefore, let's define Faith as a trusting belief in the substantial reality of GOD, as Infinite Living-MIND and man's inherent ability to access and direct this power in strict accordance with the Laws of its Being. Recall that your own subconscious mind is a personal connection to this Infinite Intelligence!

Therefore, desires, hopes and obsessions that are mixed with the emotion of faith and presented to the subconscious mind, tend to transform themselves into their physical realities. Notice the meditative or inside-out methods of prayer that Jesus used. He displayed tremendous inner strength and confidence, based on his unwavering faith in God's power and intelligence.

Study the book of Hebrews carefully considering these definitions to grasp fully the application of the principle of faith to any worthy cause. By trusting belief, Abraham established his name in history forever. He departed Ur of the Chaldeans, a prosperous city, to build a new nation from a promise.

Through faith, Joseph became the Vizier of Egypt, second only to the Pharaoh in power and responsibility. He saved many people's lives through his wisdom and prudence, including his own families.

Through faith, David became Israel's first truly successful king. He taught many people through his psalms and example, to improve the quality of their lives. Through faith, Solomon asked for wisdom and understanding to teach the ways of success in life; **which is an enduring legacy for you to use today.** Through faith, Jesus taught the wisdom and power of belief. And, profoundly changed the world forever!

There are many other examples of men and women who have won their dreams, both great and small, from life. Some have applied their faith to bring peace and freedom from the awful tyranny of oppression. While others have applied their faith to bring peace to a single family and free themselves from the awful tyranny of poverty and illiteracy.

Faith when viewed as a trusting belief in that which is trustworthy and believable is very useful. However, beliefs can be dangerous and confusing when they are not founded on universal principles and natural laws. Such as is described in this book.

"The simple *believe* every word; but the *prudent* look well to his going."
-King Solomon

History provides many examples of the hazards of "misbelief." That is sincere belief or "blind trust" in that which is not founded on correct principles and natural laws. The

Solomon's Wealth – Pharaoh's Treasures

memory of such tragedies as Jonestown and many other atrocities, seem all too recent.

The biblical definition of faith emphasizes substance and evidence for this very reason; you must recognize and use this fact. Learn to use Critical Reasoning and Knowledge to improve your understanding. That is, make careful analysis or research of things by asking pinpointed, direct questions. Read and discuss with your loved ones about the "Art of Crap detecting" in *Brain Power* by Karl Albrecht. And, you can study "Accurate Knowledge" in the *Law of Success* by Dr. Hill.

Anthony Robbins, author of *Unlimited Power* and *Awaken the Giant Within*, coaches us to change our limiting or conflicting beliefs immediately, while conditioning ourselves to sustain our achievements over time. This conditioning is essential to lasting improvements in your character and habits. Take the time to learn these principles and put them to use toward your goals now.

Also, pray for the understanding when you need to make sound judgments. James wrote in 1:5-6 "If any of you lack **wisdom**, let him *ask* of God, who gives liberally, and upbraids not, and it shall be given you. But let him ask in **faith**, nothing wavering. For the waver is like a wave of the sea driven with the wind and tossed." Study your bible, supplemented by books such as this one to better understand it's precepts and principles. This will enable you to recognize correct biblical principles.

Furthermore appropriate and personalize this Autosuggestion to help you to get more Wisdom and Faith. Remember your subconscious mind accepts instructions more readily when you are in your most relaxed state. Repeat slowly for 10 minutes a day, at least twice a day, just before bed and just after you awake-

"Wisdom, understanding and faith are my wealth; I seek them daily through the Infinite Intelligence of my subconscious mind. I exercise my hope and expectation of these qualities as much as I can, in the conduct of all my affairs. I know that my hopes shall be realized by my acting on the ideas and instructions I receive for the attainment of needs and desires. I am learning to sincerely love these principles; therefore I pray deeply through my heart's mind for them."

Adopt these steps to help unlock the door of the Wisdom of Faith:

1) Busy your mind in the search of ways to use wisdom and faith more often. Study your bible diligently, also this and the other books and tapes mentioned. You can build your **Personal Achievement Library** as you look for methods that yield the most definite value to you for the least cost; which means balancing effectiveness with efficiency. You should always try to "Do the right things, right."

2) Develop definite success reflexes by acting repetitively and immediately on the ideas and thoughts that you receive from practicing self-suggestion. These reflexes will start to come as personal statements and thoughts of inspiration such as "Just do it!"

3) Know what you want and that you will obtain it by cooperating and harmonizing with natural laws and principles. Expect your subconscious mind to aid you tremendously in your definite purposes.

4) Faithfully persist in your actions, prayers and instructions. Diligence and self-discipline are the hallmarks of achievement.

WISDOM and FAITH

Key Points to Remember

You have learned that two of the most prominent and powerful biblical success principles are wisdom and faith.   Infinite Intelligence and Power, as the substantial reality underlying these two principles, are accessed through your subconscious mind and applied according to natural laws.

You have seen that misapplication or lack of these qualities can and often lead to tragedy in life. Take heed to these precautions as you continue on your personal journey to achievement, both great and small.

You have also learned to take the time and commit yourself now to these principles. You now understand that Wisdom and Faith as proved by our key role models are the cornerstones of true wealth.

You recognize the beginning of the patterns of achievement, laid down for your use by the ancients (Hammurabi, David, Solomon, Jesus, Job) and the modern (Dr. Hill, Dr. Carver, etc.) philosophers, counselors and scientists. Observe carefully any other major achiever that you can. You will not find them lacking certain degrees of qualities of wisdom and faith.

Study your bible diligently; alongwith this and other companion books and tapes mentioned. Build and use your **Personal**

Solomon's Wealth – Pharaoh's Treasures

Achievement Library as you look for methods that yield the most definite benefits to your achievement efforts.

Specific DESIRE and PURPOSE

"To every thing there is a season, and a *time* to every **purpose** under the heaven"   - King Solomon

"Choose a job you **love**, and you will never have to work a day in your life." -Confucius

hat specifically do you want in each major area of your life? What do you dream and think about most? Are you willing to commit all of your life's energy and resources to your goals? Answer these questions honestly and accurately and you will have taken significant possession of Solomon's wealth.

A Specific Desire is an *intense want* for *something definite or certain;* whether it is intangible, such as a *state of mind* or tangible, such as *material riches*. **Specific Purpose** is the *intent, aim* and *determination* to realize the object of a particular desire. The combination of these principles causes you to focus your power and resources on the transformation of your dreams into physical reality.

Specific purpose in life is usually a personal discovery. It is the direction and intention of your life that you have uncovered for yourself. It is not something that someone can or should decide for you. My research of ancient and modern literature, suggests that this discovery will typically come from a search for definite means to *personal fulfillment*.

When you commit to a feasible, enjoyable goal, success through hard work and diligence is almost guaranteed. The random effect of chance prevents absolute guarantees.

Specific Desire is an intense, particular want or goal, and Specific Purpose is your reason or intention for your specific desire. For instance, the author attended college with the macro purpose of becoming a computer information manager. My classes, seminars and summer internships were micro goals, which lead to the realization of employment as a computer information manager. You will set and reach specific goals along the road of your major purpose in life. These definite goals and desires are your stepping stones to achievement.

The most moving example of biblical specific desire and purpose that I have read, is King David's obsession "to build a house of rest for the ark of the covenant of the LORD, and for the footstool of our GOD." It is wise to make spiritual and practical observation of this profound example of the power of specific desire and purpose.

Recall that David very diligently and sincerely meditated *a form of autosuggestion*, on the universal precepts and principles of Infinite Living-Mind or Universal Spirit. This "Living GOD," who has been called many things by men, provided David with inspiration and guidance. The second book of Samuel 7:13 reads, "He [David] shall build a house for my

Specific DESIRE and PURPOSE

name, and I will establish the throne of his kingdom forever."

Then out of both Awe and Love of GOD, David made it his heart's desire to build a house for the name of the LORD GOD. 2 Samuel 7:1,2- "And it came to pass, when the king sat in his house, and the Lord had given him rest round about from all his enemies, that the king said unto Nathan, the prophet. See, now, I dwell in a house of cedar, but the ark of GOD dwells within curtains."

However, due to the demands of war David could not build the house himself, instead he pasted his particular desire and purpose to his heir, King Solomon. 1 Chron. 28:2- "Then David the king stood up upon his feet, and said, Hear me, my brothers and people: *As for me,* I had it in mine heart to build an house of rest for the ark of the covenant of the LORD, and for the footstool of our God, and had made ready for the building: But God said unto me, you shall not build an house for my name, because you have been a man of war, and have shed blood."

Therefore, David specifically charged Solomon to "take heed **now**; for the LORD has chosen you to build a house for the sanctuary: be strong, and **do it**."- 1 Chron. 28:10.

Solomon, out of love and respect for David and God, "*determined* to build a house for the name of the LORD, and a house for his kingdom."- 2 Chron. 2:1. 1 Kings 5:5- "And behold, I *purpose* **to build an house** unto the name of the LORD my God, as the LORD spoke unto David my father, saying, Your son, whom I will set upon your throne in your room, he shall build an house unto my name."

In studying this history, you can see that by knowing what they wanted, Kings David and Solomon used all of their resources, *not the least of which being the LORD GOD himself*, to transform their desire into reality. Their particular desire was to build the house, while their particular purpose or reason was to honor GOD!

Also recognize the attitude of positive expectation which David and Solomon had they would not accept failure to build the house. You also must adopt this attitude toward your worthy goals and purposes. Dr. Hill and W. Clement Stone, Chairman of the Hill Foundation, clearly proves that a positive mental attitude is essential to success.

To focus or concentrate your resources, you must have something definite to concentrate on! *Focused energy* and *concentration* are powers that can be used to remove barriers and accomplish particular goals faster.

For instance, the energy of the sun will burn wood or paper when concentrated through a simple magnifying glass. Also, when you focus positive energy on your dreams and sustain that focus through self-discipline, you will accomplish your purpose.

Do you know what you want to be and do?

Knowing specifically what you want can be confusing because there is so much from which to choose. For instance you may want a new car, a new boat, new wardrobe, computer, a new house, more money, a new spouse and a new church all ASAP!

Fortunately, choosing your specific desires can also be very exciting. You see **your positive dreams and fantasies can be methodically transformed into reality; this is cause for celebration, hope and action!**

There are several excellent programs on the market that will help you to do this. I highly recommend two practical and fun programs: The Neuropsychology of Self-Discipline and The Neuropsychology of Achievement.

Therefore, to make the best use of these principles, use such programs to help you adopt a major mission in your life and a practical, definite plan to achieve it. The best starting point is to acknowledge that you need to know **what** you want to be and do, **why** you want it, **how** and **when** will you get it.

Remember, you have tremendous wealth of mind to use as you please. Furthermore, you have access to the powerful cosmic forces of time and habit to spend on your own dreams. You have an enormous capacity to love and share a meaningful life with someone special. This wealth, though intangible, is true wealth.

Also, remember that you can only focus your energy and power on a few things at a time. If you try to do too many things at once, you will diffuse your strength and frustrate your efforts. So, choose to accomplish those things

which are most important to your sense of
purpose and destiny.

☥ **Use the power of Questions to find your
Answers!**

Questions are powerful aides in discovering or
choosing your specific desires and major
purpose. By learning and practicing
purposeful questions, many achievers over the
ages have invented new technologies and
techniques.

The basic curiosities, desire for understanding
and rigors of human survival have proven the
value of questions. Scientist, Theologians,
Philosophers and military Strategist use
questions to uncover facts and truths. The
simple power of the four fundamental
questions What, Why, How, When, provide
an excellent starting point.

In discovering your specific purpose and
desires, you can ask **What** and **Why** oriented
questions. Such as **what** do I enjoy doing
most and **why**? **What** are my specific interest
and hobbies; **why** do I like these? When I
reflect on the moments in my life that I felt
most fulfilled, **what** was I doing and **why** was
I doing it? **What** have I always dreamed of
doing; but have not yet done and **why**?

Make a list or a personal survey with these
kinds of questions on it. Go to a quiet place
where you will not be disturbed. Repeat your
questions to yourself aloud or record them on
a tape recorder and listen thoughtfully to
them, *while fully expecting answers*. Keep

your list or tape near you until you have certain and clear answers to each of your questions.

Also, you may also ask some of your intimate relations to share their thoughts with you regarding these questions. Your specific desires will start to emerge from your study and contemplation of your answers. The time that it takes to receive answers will vary and depend on your knowledge and practice of mental laws.

As you receive answers to your questions, you will also start to receive ideas of how you can achieve your desires. Capture these ideas on paper, Dictaphone or tape recorder immediately! Good ideas are like beautiful, wild birds that appear for fleeting moments.

Remember nothing worth while comes without a price. Your only price is to use the principles of *prayer, meditation* and ***autosuggestion*** freely to help you achieve specific aims.

After using these principles for thousands of years many men and women have received enormous benefits. By impressing upon your own subconscious mind specific desires, goals and needs through prayer, meditation or autosuggestion, you are using more of your mind. This gives you a much better success rate than only using your conscious-analytical mind.

Your subjective or subconscious mind is your personal connection to the Universal Living-Mind. Universal Mind or GOD Force is available to anyone who recognizes the "God given power of thought, and uses it according to the principles of unvarying natural laws."

Consider in the light of this truth Matthew 21:22- "And all things, whatsoever you shall ask in prayer, *believing*, you shall receive." Furthermore, understand the accuracy and power of Matthew 7:7: "Ask and it shall be given you; seek, and you shall find; knock and it shall be opened unto you."

Consider this illustration of the practical value of specific direction and purpose in your life. When I was in the military we used to practice a tactical exercise called "Land Navigation." The object of the exercise is to navigate through terrain under given conditions. The conditions are that a small team of soldiers is dropped in the deep woods or another terrain. The team only has a compass, map, and radio and target destinations.

Each person in the team has a certain role to play to reach the designated areas, within a reasonable period. The team uses many skills and tools to reach the destination. For instance, the team must be capable of reading a map for particular terrain features or landmarks.

Also, the team must know how to properly orient and use a compass, while counting paces for approximate distance measures. The radio operator must exercise proper discipline and protocol when using the radio.

If a map or compass is not available the team must know how to orient their direction using the sun, moon and stars. Pacific island cultures mastered these skills in their sea faring days.

Compare the scenario of "Land Navigation" to life. **How many people have you seen wandering in the wilderness of life, without a compass, map, radio and the skills to use them or a specific destination?**

Principle based instructions and counsel is your compass specific plans of action are your maps and communication technology and techniques are your radio. Specific major purpose and desires are destinations of your own choice. Learn to love the use of this analogy to help you and your families navigate the wilderness of your life.

In setting your plan of action to realize your purpose and desires, ask **How** and **When** oriented questions. These powerful questions, when combined with the working principles of faith and autosuggestion, generate lists of ideas and methods that cause success.

Ask yourself through the principles of faith and autosuggestion such questions as: How can I use what I've learned from my parents or grandparents to help me be successful? When will I start acting on these instructions? How can I specifically use the principles of Solomon's *Wealth* to cause my success in every major area of my life? When and how can I get started? How and when can I learn and put to practical use the principles of my *Bible* which cause success and blessing; and avoid those which cause failure and defeat?

Solomon's Wealth – Pharaoh's Treasures

Use your full imagination and insight to outline a sequence of activities or behavior to develop your plans of action. Remember to plan the steps necessary to reach your dreams, fully realizing that even the best laid plans must adapt to winds of reality. When you experience temporary setbacks, adjust your plans appropriately and continue positive action toward your ***purpose***.

Positive Action here means continuing to move forward step-by-step, *thought-by-thought*, with **diligence and perseverance to your goal.** The quality of your plans and your diligence will decide the results that you see. Without practical and accurate plans, there is no positive action and without positive action there is no significance achievement.

Key Points to remember

✝ *Specific major purpose* in life is usually a personal discovery. It is the general direction and intention of your life that you have uncovered for yourself. It is not something that someone can or should decide for you.

✝ *Specific desire* is a *particular* aspiration or micro goal. Your desires may be tangible, such as a new car, boat, house or intangible, such as a more effective character, greater knowledge and energy.

✝ King David's obsession "to build a house of rest for the ark of the covenant of the LORD, and for the footstool of our GOD," is an excellent example of specific purpose and desire.

☥ Focused energy or organized effort is power that can be used to remove barriers and accomplish particular goals faster.

☥ By asking and answering relevant questions, achievers over the ages have invented new technologies and techniques for solving specific problems and exploiting good ideas. The simple power of the four fundamental questions What, Why, How and when, provide an excellent basis to start.

Counsel and Instruction

"Hear *counsel*, and receive *instruction*, that you may be wise in your latter end."
        -King Solomon

"Do not be proud on account of your knowledge;   *consult* the   ignorant and the wise."   -Ptah-Hotep

ounsel and Instructions are essential to your achievement efforts. These two principles alone can cause either success or failure. Ponder the fact that of all the information recorded since 6000 BC; most of it is instruction of some kind. These instructions range from poems about sea travel to knitting. Yes literature, music and speech have all served to instruct, counsel and teach.

King Solomon left a rich legacy of instructions or proverbs for your specific guidance. Instruction intended to teach everything from parenting to working. Solomon stated that the purpose of his proverbs is, "To know **wisdom** and **instruction**; to perceive the words of **understanding**; to receive the instruction of wisdom, justice, judgment, and equity. To give subtility to the simple, to the young man **knowledge** and **discretion**."[Pro. 1:2-4]

Also, Nebuchadnezzar, King of ancient Babylon, actively used his counselors in developing his kingdom to its greatest glory. Recall from your bible that the ancient Chaldean people, like the Egyptians, were considered very wise and learned. In support of this fact, Nebuchadnezzar chose only the most wise and skillful of the Hebrew slaves to attend his court-

"And the king spoke unto Ashpenaz, the master of his eunuchs, that he should bring *certain* of the children of Israel, and of the king's seed, and of the princes, children in whom was no blemish, but well favored, and *skillful* *in all* **wisdom**, and *gifted* in **knowledge,** and **understanding** *science* and such as had ability in them to stand in the king's palace, and whom they might *teach* the **learning** and the tongue of the Chaldeans."[Daniel 1:3-4]

Obviously, based on this and other verses Nebuchadnezzar understood the value of instruction and counsel. However, this success habit was evident before Nebuchadnezzar's reign; an earlier Babylonian king named Hammurabi provided civilization with its first recorded code of legal instructions. The underlying principles of these laws are evident in many of our modern governments, such as retribution in kind or money.

Furthermore, counsel and instruction are the very glue of democratic, capitalistic society. You are surrounded by schools, universities, churches, government agencies, private businesses and volunteer organizations; all designed explicitly to provide guidance or coaching. Recognize and value this truth and you will surely increase your ability to carry out your decisions.

Solomon's Wealth – Pharaoh's Treasures

The President of United States has chief counselors called Cabinet members. Counselors of the leaders of large businesses are Board members. Consultants provide advice, recommendations or counsel to their clients.

Everyone who has held major responsibility since the beginning of civilization required other people's knowledge and skills. The Egyptian Pharaoh's chief counselors were Viziers. These obvious facts are not to insult your intellect, rather to point out the *necessity* of sound instruction and guidance.

"Where no counsel is, the people fall; but in the multitude of counselors there is safety."
King Solomon [Pro. 11:14]

Your bible itself, in its essential element, is prudent instruction for every area of your life, including economic, social, spiritual and intellectual. It represents **Infinite Intelligence as the source** of sound guidance for principle centered living. This is a stupendous fact that this book will help you better understand and use. Give sincere appreciation to your Creator for such an invaluable tool and guiding light for life.

☥ Cooperation is good Counsel ☥

It appears that the Creator intended for men and women to cooperate in their means and methods of living. That is, human beings are social creatures by nature and are ecologically bound to one another. Your family is the first

"Natural Work Team" of which you are an integral part.

Furthermore, the bible and most other scriptural literature emphasize harmonious coexistence as a major human ideal. Carefully, observe the number of tribes in ancient Israel and the number of disciplines that Jesus organized. Each used the principle of organized effort to sustain common purposes.

What purposes and goals do you and your immediate family has in common? That is, do you have a definite major goal or purpose such as: "Everyone in our family will have a true education?" "Everyone in this family will be self-reliant enough, to contribute to the greater good of our family." "Everyone in our family will have a definite major purpose in their own life."

If you are blessed enough to have family goals and purposes like those mentioned above; you have an excellent opportunity to learn and use the principle of Synergy. Synergy, within human affairs, is the combined effort of two or more individuals, such that the total effect is greater than the sum of the individual effects.

Discuss with your loved ones the value and strength of group focus, in a spirit of mutual respect and understanding. Tell them that Andrew Carnegie used this idea to get millions of dollars and much more in spiritual wealth.

Solomon's Wealth – Pharaoh's Treasures

Tell them that *Immanuel* or Jesus the Christ *displayed* the principle of instruction, to *twelve* men, to give the world a better standard of thought and conduct. Tell them that your entire family will benefit when everyone in the family focuses their energies and resources on the good of the family as a whole.

Adapt and personalize these instructions for your family and conditions:
1) **Arrange** a meeting with your family to discuss your common goals and purposes.

2) **List** the needs and desires that you have on a clean sheet of paper, preferably a chart pad. What does each of you want need and ought to have or do? What does each of you want for the family? Stay loose and creative with this list; anything goes! The only criterion you might follow is that the list is reasonable and humanly possible.

Use prayer and autosuggestion to seek worthy goals and purposes for your family from Infinite Intelligence.

3) **Discuss** the list openly, practicing the habits of "seeking first to understand, then to be understood." Listen with your ears and mind, also your eyes; pay attention to body language and facial expressions. If you sense discomfort, patiently seek to understand the sources of the discomfort-- "I sense that you feel a little uncomfortable with something that I just said or did. Would you like to discuss it further?" Look for commonalty in the items. Are some items paraphrases or restatements of others? If so, consolidate these items into one.

4) **Choose** the items from the consolidated list which feel very important and urgent. That is, those goals which **must be done now to avoid major crises in the near future**. Then, take one or two items which feel most important, but not urgent. These goals should be broader and more preventive in nature. Such as, a family **personal Purpose statement** or a family **Code of Personal Conduct**.

5) **Commit** yourselves to your choices, remembering that flexibility makes any plan realistic. If your conditions change, just adjust your plans. However, be sure that you maintain the spirit or intent of your plan. Self-Discipline, perseverance, persistent and faith will be your greatest assets in aiding you to realize your goals.

The principles of Counsel and Instruction are major premises of synergy. This is the very reason committees, boards, cabinets and teams are so much more effective than any individual working alone. The power and potential of synergistic business operations have fueled many a merger and produced tremendous wealth.

Therefore, when you participate in activities related to your specific purpose, remember the prerequisites: cooperation, mutual respect and understanding; apply the Golden Rule and think "Win/Win."

Principled Based Instruction and **counsel** are major leverages for winning your dreams. Cultivate the habit of recognizing biblical

principles in the instruction that you receive.
And, describe the principles of the instruction
that you may give.

If you have ever followed the instructions to
bake an Apple Pie; then you got a delicious
apple pie when you finished. Otherwise, the
instructions or ingredients were faulty. The
instructions or recipe worked because they are
based on the correct procedures for baking an
apple pie. This simple example shows the
value of finding and following good
instructions. You can surely see that diligence
in following principle based instructions
causes **"sweet success."**

When you observe people who are successful
in their chosen fields, acknowledge to yourself
that they followed, adapted or created the
instructions and *guidance* that resulted in their
success! For instance, medical doctors go to
school for approximately seven to eight years,
study and learn their field; then, pass their
license examinations.

Seek and use the counsel of qualified people
available to you. Cultivate relationships with
people whose advice you respect. Mentors,
spouses, teachers, preachers and friends can
all be excellent sources of good counsel.
However, remember there is no substitute for
your personal responsibility to choose your
actions and thoughts.

I have found that an excellent way to attract
and keep mentors is to follow or at least try
their counsel immediately. This is equally true
for your loved ones; when you seek and use
their advice, you improve the relationship.

COUNSEL and INSTRUCTION

Everyone likes to feel appreciated and *will gravitate to sources of appreciation*. Ensure that you are satisfied however, that the advice is based on sound principles and accurate knowledge. Teach this to your children in their youth and it will serve them well all of their lives.

"Hear, you children, the *instruction* of a father and *attend* to know understanding."
King Solomon [Pro. 4:1]

Search out and observe any person who is currently doing that which you want to do or who has the character, values and habits which you desire to have. Ask yourself expectantly -- *"What principles and teachings are they using; what Biblical teaching or personal experience is being applied?" "What characteristics and habits are they exercising to reach these goals and mental states?"* If you can verify your observations with the individual through personal contact, you can ask them for the source of their instructions (methods and means) and direction in life.

Key Points to remember

You have learned that instruction and counsel has been the prevailing intent of organized knowledge since the beginning of civilization. Men and women have gathered and used these principles to get the methods and means by which they can succeed and survive. The volumes of this guidance and advice are so numerous that you are hard pressed to see it all at once in your mind.

You are more aware of the importance and value of instruction and counsel, as the basis of many of our oldest institutions, including the family. Successful Kings and Presidents have exercised these truths for obtaining their purposes throughout the ages. Similarly, families who consult and instruct each other, based on mutual respect and understanding greatly enrich the quality of their lives.

Finally, you have a practical exercise that you may appropriate and adapt for practicing organized effort or Synergy with your own "Natural Work Team."

Prudence and Discretion

"To give subtility to the simple, to the young man   *knowledge* and *discretion*."   - King Solomon

"Woe unto them that are wise in their own eyes, and **prudent** in their own sight!"   - Isaiah 5:21

Prudence and **Discretion** or *sound judgment* and *careful thought* are very pragmatic biblical success principles. Prudence is the quality of sound judgment in practical matters, cautious in one's conduct or behavior. And, discretion is the quality of being careful about what, when and how one conducts himself or herself; caution; Prudence. The biblical use of the word Prudence describes a person of discretion in their *attitude and treatment* of knowledge or understanding.

These are application principles of **Wisdom** and **Understanding.** King Solomon wrote [Pro. 8:12] - "I *wisdom* dwells with *Prudence*, and find out knowledge of witty inventions." He also wrote [Pro. 18:15] - "The heart of the prudent gets knowledge; and the ear of the wise seeks knowledge." In short, it is wise to develop and exercise Prudence.

The Law of Choice is that every act is either a conscious or preconscious choice, whether to act or to think. Therefore, consider the wisdom of the Creator in giving you practical means to discern *cause* and *effect*, thus the chance to choose those things that *cause* the *effects* that you need and want most.

Prudence and discretion are the working principles or the means you shall use to decide between alternatives. This is important, because some things that you may desire, which are tangible to your five senses, require balance, restraint and context.

You can balance the single minded pursuit of material possession, with enduring gratitude and desire of healthy states of mind such as: Peace, harmony, tranquillity, or enthusiasm. That is to say, material possessions should not be our primary focus and only purpose. When they are, we tend to experience disappointments in the deeper sides of human experience.

Over indulgence in material things, including sex and other acts, has destroyed many a wayfarer in life. Oddly, intemperance with anything that is pleasurable to the senses tends toward tragedy and frustration.

Whosoever is not aware of the perils of overeating, over drinking and boundless pleasure seeking; Let him consider the latter end of such people as King Henry VIII and some modern celebrities. These were people who lost much more than fortunes in gold and opportunity, to undisciplined desires, running rampant in their lives.

Your five basic senses are your means of detecting and responding to your physical environment. However, what about your nonphysical or intangible environment; how do you detect and respond to it? Your power to *think* is the sixth sense that you use for such realities. You'll learn more about thought in a later chapter, for now *think* about Prudence.

As Emerson reflected on prudence, he observed that proficiency in knowledge of the world varies by degrees. He spotlighted three particular classes of views concerning this subject.

The first class lives for the use of *symbols* [Material Possessions], esteeming health and wealth a *final* good. This class of proficiency is how the vast majority of people concentrate their energies; therefore, making it difficult for them to recognize the greater realities underlying the objects and symbols.

The second class exercises a higher consciousness of the *beauty* of the symbol; such as the poet, artist, *naturalist* and *scientist*. Our annals of recorded history represent considerable evidence for confirmation of Emerson's conclusions. There is beauty inherent in all of nature; however, there are various degrees of appreciation.

The third class lives above the beauty of the symbol to the *beauty of the thing* signified [Virtues, Principles, Natural Laws, Universal Cosmic Truths]; Emerson called these wise. Undoubtedly, substantial reality exists far beyond conscious detection. Invisible scales of color, light, vibration and thought are but a few examples of this truth.

Solomon's Wealth – Pharaoh's Treasures

Jesus, as a historical figure, apparently exercised Prudence and discretion in the heights of the third class. Paul testifies of him in Ephesians 1:8- "In whom we have redemption through his blood, the forgiveness of sins, according to the *riches of his grace*; In which he has abounded toward us in *all* **wisdom and Prudence."**

However, take careful notes that in some degree symbols, when used as tools or means instead of ends, are both necessary and prudent. Try not paying your bills or saving and investing your money if you don't understand this point.

Everyone must, by the rules of economic conduct, provide or have provided for them water, food, clothing, shelter and protection. Otherwise, they cannot survive. The human mind will do far more to avoid this tragedy than to gain a million wants and desires. Each of these needs has a cost and is not free; each consumes resources- money, time and energy. Each must be met before one can progress to the higher planes of Prudence in life.

"Success is a matter of habit."

You can plainly see the practical value of Prudence and discretion in the administration of financial and social affairs. This is where the Law of Habit Force can come to your aid.

Habit Force conditions your mind and body to sustain a particular pattern of thought and action. Repetitions of a particular activity or thought will *cause* you to feel the impulse or tug of habit force. If you are not yet sure about this fact, drive to work every day over the same route. You will soon find that when you leave your driveway you will automatically turn toward work; unless you are aware of where you're going.

Therefore you have the opportunity to use this force to apply Prudence to your habit of saving and investing your **Time** and **Money**. Saving and investing time and money is essential to your effort to win your dreams from life.

Most people have experienced, at least once, the urgent need for immediate cash. Whatever the cause or purpose of the need, whether it was to help a friend, loved one or themselves. If finances flowed in along with Prudence and discretion, then they were better prepared for the uncertainty. However, if money flowed in, hotly pursued by the poverty consciousness, covetousness, jealousy, and undisciplined greed; whosoever was in need stayed in need. *Study for spiritual understanding all that the Word of God teaches concerning money.*

I believe that the **habit** *of saving and investing money is more valuable than all the money that you can save or invest.* Consider the virtues of this habit, it *causes*- 1) Your money to work for you; instead of you working for it, 2) peace of mind and a sense of independence, 3) the development of self-discipline, which can be used in other areas of life, 4) the ability to take advantage of opportunities requiring cash, 5) and the ability to give appropriate financial help to the needy.

Solomon's Wealth – Pharaoh's Treasures

Observe my emphasis on both saving and investing; it is very prudent to do both. Saving money generally means you are allowing someone else to use your money. Savings and Loans, Credit Unions and other financial institution will pay you a small percentage for the privilege of keeping your money, but charge you a higher fee for the privilege of lending it to you. You can consider this the price of security.

In contrast, although investing your money has varying risk; it's generally a better deal. The idea of investing is to purchase a sound (prudent) investment at low cost and sell it for a profit, generally the higher the risk, the more profit you can earn. Conversely, when your risks are low, your profits are low.
****

Remember money is a tool or means, not an end in itself! Recognize, to your personal benefit, that after Dr. Hill spent **twenty-five years** studying the *causes of economic success*; He lists money **last** of twelve enduring forms of riches. Wisdom exclaimed through Solomon- "Receive my *instruction* and not silver; and *knowledge* rather than choice gold."

You must save and invest money for your definite major purpose, whatsoever it maybe. However, as a tool the possession of money or any other material thing must not take precedent over human need for shelter, clothing, food and protection. If your loved ones urgently request your saving and investment for any one of these, my counsel is to invest in the Laws of Compensation and Increasing Returns. And remember when these four basic needs are not fulfilled human beings cannot live.

However, Prudence will instruct us to ensure that our aide is not a permanent crutch. It has been wisely stated- **"Give a man a fish and you feed him for a day. Teach him how to fish and you feed him for a lifetime."** The main point is in matters of dire need, give willingly of your substance or "fish"; in matters of principle, give more vigorously of your example and instruction.

The habit of savings and investing your Time and is undoubtedly as valuable and necessary as saving your money. Through this habit you will exercise more discretion, as you pursue your definite purpose and goals.
Time is accessible to you for a finite period, in practical day-to-day terms. No one has unlimited amounts of this precious wealth; which is infinitely more valuable than money.Therefore, you must spend your time effectively to achieve your goals and dreams.

☥ Cultivate the Habit of Preparation and Planning

Preparation and Planning have remained crucial elements of success from our ancient past until today. "Ponder the path of your feet and let all your ways be established" wrote Solomon [Pro. 4:26]. Recall the intricate preparations of rituals and rites described in historical texts, including your bible. The offerings and supplications were prepared to definite specifications.

Solomon's Wealth – Pharaoh's Treasures

No lasting achievement in life has ever been the result of haphazard and undisciplined activities. King David made **definite plans** to build the Lord a house, by **preparing** wood and other essential materials. Imhotep made **definite plans** to build Pharaoh a monument, by careful engineering and science. President Kennedy made definite plans to see Americans on the moon, by supporting fiscal and scientific preparations.

Definite Plans, as stated in the previous chapters, represents your road map to conduct yourself according to your definite purpose and desires. Therefore, invest energy in those people or things which are *important* and *relevant* in helping you. Remember to do it now and do it right!

As you exercise the power and responsibility of Volition, be careful not to expose your subconscious mind to people or influences which are not conducive your goals. Consciously use the Law of Attraction by surrounding yourself with influences that *cause* or compel you to achievement habits.

Therefore, remember avoid sharing information about your major goal with people who display general tendencies of jealousy, arrogance, conceit and mischief. "A talebearer reveals secrets, but he that is of a faithful spirit conceals the matter," Solomon explained.

PRUDENCE and DISCRETION

Key Points and Quotes to remember

Prudence and discretion are practical applications of wisdom and understanding, based on the Law of Choice. The word prudent is used in the bible to describe a person of discretion in their attitudes and treatment of knowledge and understanding.

Prudent decisions and actions are essential to your success. The habits of saving and investing time and money with discretion are necessary to cultivate success.

"The heart of the **prudent** gets knowledge; and the ear of the wise seek knowledge." King Solomon proverbs 18:15

"**Discretion** shall preserve you, understanding shall keep you"
King Solomon proverbs 2:11.

THOUGHTS are TOOLS,
MIND over Matter

"The **thoughts** of the *diligent* tend only to
    plenteousness; but of every one that is
hasty, only to want."
-King Solomon

"Technology is to the *Body*, as the *Body* is to
the **Mind**."

                     -Jahbril

Solomoses

Technologies, both *physical* and *mental*, are tools designed for specific applications. And, the combination of human thought and tools is one of the most important applications of the Mind of Man. It's through this application that humankind has manifested great powers to both destroy and construct civilization.

Archeologists have shown that early man distinguished himself in the development and use of tools. For instance, stone and wood were used to make axes, bows, arrows and spears. Ancient peoples used such tools to gather food, clothing and shelter from wild animals and the elements.

In reflecting on the impact tools on accomplishment, it's easy to overlook the profound impact of the first and most powerful technology at our disposal. Your body is an organic tool, with *design purpose, under the direction of the "I AM that You Are."* In particular, your brain and nervous system is highly sophisticated, organic technology. In fact, computer technology is capable of replicating, to some extent, such processes as memory recall, language and voice recognition.

The *creative power* of thought processes is the origin and means by which we have brought the earth's available resources into service. Study "The Edinburgh Lectures of Mental Science" and "Bible Mystery, Bible Meaning" by Thomas Troward for more in-depth knowledge of this subject. **Do not neglect to learn about the creative power inherent in your thought; this is a very practical and profound necessity!**

Chapter one describes the methods by which you may tap the power of your *subconscious mind* to generate ideas, solve-problems and make decisions. **Imagination** and *thought*, **technology** and "*smart work*" will *transform* your **ideas** into *reality*, **problems** into *solutions* and **decisions** into *destiny*.

Today's uses of tools and techniques mark a significant milestone in the development and use of the human mind. Our technologies have enabled us to comprehend more, faster than ever before. Physical tools and technologies are extensions of your hands and feet, extending the effects of your labor. Therefore, you can plant and harvest food crops faster with mechanical tools, than you could by hand.

The application of technology to thoughts and ideas has built sprawling ancient cities and nations, such as Babylon, Thebes, Ur,

Solomon's Wealth – Pharaoh's Treasures

Rameses and Pithom. Archaeological finds revealed tremendous architecture and attention to detail in these cities. The Great Pyramids in Egypt uncovered a masterful combination of the power of human ingenuity and the technology of that particular age.

Every major age in the recorded history of man, uncovered the advantages of possessing technologically advanced tools of that age. For instance, the use of fire made humans far more powerful than other animals. Suddenly Man could remove unwanted vegetation, cook food, warm shelters and better protect himself.

The same observation has been true in the conduct of wars between nations. Whichever army has blended technological advantage with advanced mental tactics, has usually won.

Enormous quantities of evidence to support this fact have been uncovered in many caves, tombs and monuments of antiquity. Egyptian hieroglyphics display engineers and laborers employing advanced techniques in art, war and construction.

"First the Thought, then the Thing."

Upon close consideration you may recognize the fact that before anything is created through the labor of the body or the use of tools, *it is first created in the mind*. For example, before Imhotep had laid one brick on the famous Step Pyramid, he developed an idea or a blueprint of the final structure in his mind. He then transported this blueprint into building instructions. Whereon, he *combined these* *initial representations of his **thoughts** with the best **tools** and **technologies** available in his age, and by that **transforming** his idea into physical reality.*

Before Garrett A. Morgan developed the first Traffic Light, he had a clear idea of it in his mind. He transformed this idea into blueprints and instructions, by that allowing the invention to be manufactured into physical reality. You see so many traffic lights today that it's very easy to forget their value.

Charles Drew first conceived of the idea and the method to store human blood in "blood banks" in his mind. By that saving countless lives over many years of war and disease. He transformed his thought from an idea into a physical reality.

Today you can observe hundreds of inventions or ideas that have been transformed into reality. Watch such programs as Beyond 2000 and Invention for many more examples. What does your television set, telephone, place of employment and your house has in common? All these items began in someone's mind as a thought!

Technology is a powerful instrument of **Cause** and **Achievement™**. That is, transforming ideas or opportunities into achievement of specific desire and purpose. Before you can fully grasp the process of transforming ideas and opportunities into their physical values, you will benefit from a practical understanding of what is meant by terms idea and opportunity.

Solomon's Wealth – Pharaoh's Treasures

An idea is a thought or mental conception of a plan, intention or action. In other words, an idea is mental appearance of something specific. And, when you focus your power of attention-awareness on your inner screen of consciousness, you can see ideas in sensory rich detail. Ideas are generated in the faculty of imagination and creativity. You can create images and visions of vivid detail using your imagination. Furthermore, ideas can be planted in your imagination and shared by other people, or stimulated by some event that you experience.

For instance, go to a quiet spot, where you can not be disturbed for five minutes. Close your eyes to see with your mind's eye and to listen with your heart. See in your mind the favorite romantic scenes with your spouse or "chosen one." Remember the enticing aroma of perfumes and colognes. Picture the alluring sight of one so beautiful as your friend.

Enjoy again the enchanting surroundings that collaborated with your soul to steal away your heart. Relive the warm embrace and the tingling of your nature. Passion and emotion spoken without words; songs of passion murmured but unheard. Remember the first light of the morning after. Was the nightingale your messenger of the reality of this unforgettable dream?

How does it feel, this DEJA VU? Did you feel some of the familiar emotion of those magical moments? Use the power of your imagination to see, feel, touch, taste and smell the object of your definite desire. This will create a more realistic sensation and obsession for the desire.

Opportunity is a combination of favorable circumstances for the accomplishment of your definite purpose and desires. Conditions are opportune when they are available at the right time.

Opportunity can be **uncovered**, as in new markets or **created**, as in starting your own business. In either regard, opportunity is necessary to win your goals and dreams. Exercising the principles of Solomon's Wealth will definitely help you to recognize opportunity and capitalize on it.

To initiate the process of **Cause** and **Achievement**™, you should **READ** as much as you can. That is, you should: **Recognize** the *principles* which cause success, whenever you are gathering information or learning about your major purpose and desires. Careful study and application of the principles of Solomon's Wealth, the Bible and other works from your PAL will prove invaluable.

Expect to achieve the object of your purpose and desires. A strong expectation, based on the biblical *principle of faith,* backed by *diligence* and hard work, will be accomplished. Use the principles of autosuggestion to confirm your expectations of true and enduring success.

Act on your expectation to transform your thoughts, ideas and opportunities into permanent improvement in your life. There is no substitute for **diligent action** in accomplishing major goals or life purposes. You must spend your energy and time wisely to be sure of success. ***Stay alert to the opportunity to work "smarter" by using appropriate tools and technologies.*** Such as, computers, dictating devices, tape recorders, etc.

<u>Desire</u> permanent improvements in the quality of your character and life. A strong desire or obsession for permanency of the benefits of your good ideas and opportunities helps to institute them in your life. Recall from Napoleon Hill's research that a burning desire, particularly one which consciously makes use of habit force, will cause you to succeed.

"Buy the truth, and sell it not; also wisdom, and instruction, and understanding."
-King Solomon 23:23

Reading and other forms of gathering information have been a vital part of civilization for thousands of years. Ancient artifacts reveal a tremendous amount of written literature, on stones, paper and wood. The volumes of hieroglyphs uncovered in ancient Egypt, attest to the importance of information gathering and true learning.

A major purpose for reading and learning is to increase the quality of life. And, quality of life typically increases with the amount of true education a person has. It is a broadly known fact that those who have capitalized on education, whether through school or self-taught, earn higher wages and more benefits.

THOUGHTS are TOOLS

Learning to use your thoughts along with available technologies is essential too continually improving the quality of your life. You can do this by deliberately turning your ideas and opportunities into wealth of character, mind and material.

The following formula is offered to you for your personal success. Think about its sequence and contents until you feel you understand it. Ideas and opportunities are transformed when **A^5[A to the fifth]=Achievement**:

Attitude x Attention-Awareness x Acquisition x Arrangement x Application-Assimilation = Achievement

Attitude is an enormous power to direct toward your achievement efforts. Simply stated, the more positive your feelings or emotions toward your desires, then the more likely you are to live them. It is a fundamental truth that "your attitude determines your altitude." Study and apply Dr. Hill and W. Clement Stone's *Success Through a Positive Mental Attitude*.

Attention-Awareness is the thought process by which your mind attempts to understand and focus the world around you, internally and externally. Are you aware of what you are thinking right now? Is your mind on this line or somewhere else? Make it a point to deliberately focus your attention from an inside-out point of view.

That is, listen in on your own thoughts for positive and constructive ideas; then deliberately observe and acknowledge what you are doing. If your actions are in harmony with your thoughts and major desires, you are on purpose. If not, remember only practice will make perfect.

Practice focusing your attention and conscious awareness on your specific desires or purpose with balanced consistency. That is, consciously direct your sight, hearing, speech and thought on the things that you love, desire and need. Develop the habit of periodically inventorying your attention and awareness.

Ask yourself: Where are my feet and hands in relation to where they must be to accomplish my goal? What am I physically doing vs. what I must do to succeed? What am I thinking about most of the time vs. what I must think about to succeed? What images dominate my mind's eye?

You couldn't do this always; so remember to relax your attention from time to time. The point being to ensure that your Voluntary *Attention* and *Awareness* are dominated by the physical and mental actions which cause your desires and goals.

This will help you to cultivate a positive attitude toward your major interest. Also, this will help keep your physical and mental attention-awareness off of the things that you do not want!

Always write down or otherwise record what you consider good opportunities or ideas. Keep all five of your senses on alert for opportunities to progress your purpose.

THOUGHTS are TOOLS

Informative reading, viewing and listening will uncover several opportunities. Adapt your selection of books, television programs and music to those which are closely related to your purpose. These are very important instructions to identifying or recognizing valuable opportunities; do not neglect them.

"Get wisdom, get understanding; forget it not, neither decline from the words of my mouth."   *-King David*

Acquisition of more pertinent information about the idea or opportunity that you wish to transform is the vital next step in the process. Competence and curiosity will help you to explore the feasibility of your opportunity. Purposely develop the use of your **PAL** and mentors or role models.

Learn to love learning new things about your purpose and desires. Research and experiment with your definite ideas and opportunities. This will help prevent costly errors in judgment. You do not need to conduct scientifically precise research and experimentation, unless you are a scientist.

Arrange or organize what you have learned about your opportunities and ideas into *practical* plans. Definite plans represent a significant step in the transformation process; because plans are nothing more than your thoughts translated into potential behavior and actions. These planned or potential actions must be accurate and appropriate for your purposes. For instance, if you planned to go to the bank by 3:30; but instead you went to the movie theater, your actions did not carry you to the bank.

Application or acting on your definite plans will you helps **Assimilate** ideas and opportunities into successful habits. *"Power is knowledge in motion."* Until you cultivate the habit of diligently doing the things that you know will cause achievement, you cannot accomplish your purpose and desire.

Action, action and more action are the vital link to success in any field you may attempt. The principles of self-discipline, diligence and determination are powerful action principles which will propel you to success.

The mind of humankind has created enormous inventions and achievement. Mind and machine are an awesome combination for you to use to win your goals and desires. Technology, both large and small, can definitely increase your efficiency and extend your capacity to act on your thoughts. Use appropriate technology and tools to help you and your loved ones accomplish meaningful goals.

Key Points to remember

☥ Four of the most extensive tools ever used to obtain the thoughts of man are the wheel, water, fire and electricity. These resources have been of enormous value, when harmoniously combined with human thought and determination.

THOUGHTS are TOOLS

✝ Your own mind and brain are undoubtedly your most potent and available asset; invest it most wisely. Your mind and brain is a highly sophisticated computer. Human thought processes harnessed the power of the elements and environment to build this modern age. Perhaps, we will yet succeed in applying our ingenuity similarly in saving our planet and preserving a quality life for all living things.

✝ Tools and technologies are extensions of your hands and feet, extending the effects of your labor. Therefore, you can plant crops faster with a mechanical planter, than by hand. Learn to use any tool that will be helpful to you in winning your major purpose from life.

✝ Technology, when used as a tool, is a powerful instrument of Idea and Opportunity transformation. Ideas and opportunities, like gold ore, are useless and wasted unless you mine, refine and convert them into a useful state. **READ** for understanding and knowledge. Use the A^5 formula to practice systematically realizing your definite desires.

Diligence, Determination and Focused Action

"See you a man **diligent** in his business? He shall stand before kings; he shall not stand before mean men."

-King Solomon

"**Determination** and **Focused Action** are to *achievement* as Sun and Water are to the Oak."

-Jahbril

Solomoses

ongratulations, you have arrived at a major step in the pragmatic use of Solomon's Wealth! The principles set forth in this chapter focus on *doing*, *practicing*, or taking personal **action** to *cause* your success. They are crucial to transforming your ideas into opportunities, and opportunities into success. For this the reason, I refer to these particular principles as the Action Principles.

Diligence, Determination and Focused Action combine all of the previous principles into the self-discipline you need to cause *your success*. "Indeed, to dream is to want; however, to do is to be." "The soul of the sluggard desires, and has nothing"; exclaims Solomon" but the soul of the **diligent** shall be made fat." Conscious application of action principles allows you to direct Habit Force in your favor.

Diligence, Determination and Focused ACTION

Universal Force of Habit engraves the results of every action that dominates your activities into your brain and nervous system. This establishes patterns of behavior and thoughts necessary to satisfy the **reason or cause** of your actions. For instance, by the simple acts of cleaning your teeth, washing yourself and other morning rituals you have established distinct habits of good hygiene. Force of habit causes you to do this automatically; it is very rare if ever that you will forget to brush your teeth.

Likewise, diligent practice will perfect a golf swing, using the same working principle which perfects the Earth's orbit around the Sun. Remember, your character is simply the sum of your habitual thoughts and deeds. **Consistent repetition of the thoughts and actions which have caused success for thousands of years, will engrave achievement into your character!**

Therefore, all the previous Mental and Spiritual principles of Solomon's Wealth have no practical value to you without personal commitment. If you will use your PAL to develop and focus the necessary skills, attitudes and habits you will become more goal-oriented. Thus, you will better maintain or sustain your commitment. Observation reveals that many historical role models exemplified the virtues of being goal-oriented and committed to their goals.

King Solomon showed enormous determination and commitment to the purpose of his literary career. "And he spoke 3000 proverbs, and his songs were 1005." Also,

Solomon's Wealth – Pharaoh's Treasures

Solomon proved that unique virtue of diligent nature observation- "And he spoke of trees, from the cedar tree that is in Lebanon even unto the hyssop that springs out of the wall; he spoke also of beasts, and of fowl, and of creeping things, and of fish."[1 Kings 4:32, 33]

Without persistence and perseverance George W. Carver could not have caused hundreds of practical uses of such products as peanuts, potatoes, pecans and soybeans. He gave thousands of hours of concentrated thought and effort to yield such achievements. Therefore, we can enjoy Peanut butter, Mayonnaise and other synthetic products of Dr. Carver's determination.

Without exercising these qualities, you cannot make conscious use of the power of Habit Force available to you. Repetition is the key to setting up habit patterns. Only your diligence and perseverance will provide enough repetitions to condition your mental muscles or program proven success habits into your "Personal Computer."

Careful study of the lives of such historical and modern achievers as Imhotep, King David, Herodotus, Ben Franklin, Marcus Garvey and Martin L. King reveal several key success characteristics and habits. However, the most common habit that I have seen in my research of these lives is diligent action and personal commitment toward specific goals. This means that they did not accept the inevitable temporary defeats as complete failure, and always maintained a certain *Constancy of Focus.*

Your bible illustrates this point in the books of Samuel, Kings and Chronicles as it describes the many trials and triumphs of King David. Recall that David had to endure the attempted murder of his predecessor, King Saul, also his own son Absalom. However, the King remained on track and diligent in the pursuit of his major purpose and desires.

☥ "Choose your Habits; Choose your Destiny."

What better starting points for you to consciously use the power of Habit Force and the action principles than learning to build success habits and reflexes? I define success habits as a pattern of behavior engraved in your mind and causes positive and constructive achievement. Similarly, success reflexes are positive, automatic reactions that you have in response to an idea, opportunity or situation favorable to your purpose.

As you might imagine, historical experience has provided a list of specific habits and principles that cause positive results. I would like to summarize some of these as the *Ps and Os of Achievement*. They are as follows: **Prayer, Practice, Persistence, Perseverance, Potential, Purpose, Patience, Plan, Proactivity, Prioritization, Principle, Productivity, Proficiency, Positivism, Preparation** and *Organization, Observation, Optimization, Open mindedness, Opportunity and Question*. Try to think of more **Ps** and **Os** that you can apply to your dreams.

Solomon's Wealth – Pharaoh's Treasures

The power of the Ps and Os is in the intelligent application of them to your specific desires and purpose. Therefore, learn to use them to craft your habits, attitudes and behavior. Some specific habits and reflexes that you might like to develop could be:

1. **Listening actively and empathically to your**
spouse or children.
2. *Being prepared for every business presentation or*
meeting.
3. **Proactively managing your use of time, to spend**
it with your family.
4. *Studying and applying the principles of books,*
magazines or television documentaries useful to
your purpose.
5. **Not interrupting others in conversation.**
6. *Making all important decisions for yourself.*
7. **Consistently balancing your checking account**
and monitoring your investments.
8. *Exercising frequently and safely.*
9. **Eating for health and energy.**
10. *Praying and meditating consistently.*

Make liberal and creative use of Ps and Os in replacing old, self-limiting habits with success habits. Such noted experts as Karl Albrecht, Stephen Covey, Napoleon Hill, and Anthony Robbins have pointed out that to change a limiting habit or belief; you must first offer your brain a better alternative pattern. Otherwise, you will always revert to the limitation. Many unsuccessful dieters, drug, sex and alcohol abusers can painfully relate to this. Please, learn to master the principles of self-suggestion to reach your powerful subconscious mind.

The more positive your attitude and enthusiasm for the new pattern, the faster you will replace the old pattern. In describing the Pain-Pleasure principle in human nature, Anthony Robbins points out that your brain will do more to avoid or get rid of negative experiences, than it will to gain positive experiences. Therefore, he emphatically instructs you to associate pain to your old habit and dwell on the benefits of your new habits. Thus, pushing your own brain away from the limitation and pulling it toward the invigoration of achievement and success.

From the ancient Egyptian Imhotep to the modern legacy of Napoleon Hill, clearly persistent, character and habit building are essential to the goal-directed achiever. Therefore, without constancy of focus, any new behavior that you may wish to cause your success will remain a wish.

To install success habits and reflexes, I have personalized these guidelines into a four-step process that I call the **RAPP**; which I'd like to invite you to use and personalize further for your benefit. **RAPP** is an acronym for these four principles of habit forming: *Recognition, Attitude,* **Practice** and **Persistence**.

<u>R</u>ecognize clearly, both the old habit and the new habit that you need to exchange. Use a *Stop, Start and Continue* format in stating your intention. Be as specific and positive as

you can; Say "I *am* going to **stop** smoking now," "I *am* going to **start** my exercise program now and **continue** it from this point forward." This specifically gives your brain something on which to act. You have a much better chance of success when you can pinpoint or isolate the behavior and thoughts in question.

Attitude is very important to convincing your brain to submit the new habit as the necessary replacement of the old, limiting pattern. Faith, self-confidence, enthusiasm, desire and a positive expectation when blended through the principle of autosuggestion, will provide your mind with a powerful persuasion to adopt your conscious choice of habit.

A positive attitude helps to overcome the powerful urge and pull of the force of the old habit. To illustrate, imagine that habit force is the force of gravity and you want to reach your dreams on mars. You must first have enough energy and thrust to escape the pull of the earth's gravity, before you can reach mars. Recognize also, that the same force of gravity which you must overcome to leave Earth; you must use to land safely on mars. Similarly, you must overcome the pull of habit force in escaping from the limiting pattern. And, consciously use habit force to pull you toward the positive pattern.

Set a definite period, days or weeks depending on the habit, in which you are going to deliberately catch yourself thinking about or displaying the behavior that you want to exchange. **Focus your sense of Awareness-**

Diligence, Determination and Focused ACTION

Attention on the goals and causes of the habits that you wish to obtain.

Immediately remind yourself of all the negative short and long-term consequences of continuing. Be specific and graphic; use your imagination and all of your five senses. See and feel the painful emotions. Hear the cries of loved ones, due to your lack of effort to improve right now. What will your lives be like if you do not change now?

Also, visualize and meditate on all of the benefits and rewards of the new habit. Again, use your God given power of imagination and all of your five senses. Keep in mind that you are systematically developing the mental attitude that you will need to complete your habit formation.

_P_ractice is the act of repetition **_required_** _to_ engrave or program the new habit into your mind. Patience, persistence and effort are essential to this step. As a general guideline, it takes about three to four weeks of concerted effort to consciously build a habit. Therefore consistently act out or repeat the new behavior or thought that you wish to habituate.

One of my personal reflexes is T^2L^2, [T-squared, L-squared] which means _T_alk to _T_each, Listen to _L_earn. It is widely understood and accepted that teaching anything helps the teacher to learn more deeply. However, in the "**Talking**" half of this reflex, focus on the constructive and positive power of _questions_ to direct the creative power of your thought. As you become more skilled at listening for answers you will improve your chances of winning your goals.

Listening is a powerful means of increasing the knowledge and understanding pertinent to your goals. The "Art of Listening" is truly a skill worth cultivating and teaching to your children or other loved ones. It is applicable to personal interaction in business, education and family.

The Art of Listening involves cultivating opened minded, empathic focus of attention-awareness. That is, the more you practice attuning yourself to both inner and outer stimuli, people or circumstances the more competent and confident you become in your response. Think about how many business relationships, personal and social relationships could be improved if every one cultivated this talent.

Such mental success reflexes or trigger phrases are awesome interpersonal tools. Particularly, the habit of empathic listening and all of the "Seven Basic Habits of Highly Effective People," organized and shared by Dr. Stephen Covey.

Persistence and perseverance are essential in maintaining your conditioning of the habits and reflexes, which you develop. Will-Power, desire and determination are the necessary elements of this step. Remember the universal natural law of Utility; if you don't use it, you'll lose it. Exercise your **Desire** and **Will-power** to realize the personal rewards of the permanent use of your new habits and reflexes. Take some time, once a year at minimum, to inventory your habitual thought and actions. Use people to help you do this who can be open and honest with you. Observe any correlation or relationship between the circumstances of life and your personal habits and characteristics.

As you can see, diligent effort and labor are the fuels which will propel you to your definite desires and aspirations. Concentration and focus of this energy increase its power and the speed at which you reach your dreams. Recall that the power of a Laser light is in its concentration.

☥ Energy and ACTION ☥

In the physical sciences power introduces a time element into work. That is, power is the amount or quantity of work divided by the time required to complete the work. Therefore, we shall presently define **Personal Power** as your *capacity or energy available* to do the work required to obtain your goals within the desired time.

Therefore, your personal power increases in effect when concentrated on your goals through Focused Action and the principle of Constancy of Focus. To be clear, Constancy of Focus here means diligent, persistent action, that is sustained and adapted until the object or purpose of the action is realized. This focused action is the means by which you shall express your definite plans for causing the achievement of your purpose and desires. It makes use of Dr. Deming's world famous principle of Total Quality, **Constancy of Purpose**.

Solomon's Wealth – Pharaoh's Treasures

First however, it is important that you have a good grasp on the critical role of <u>energy</u> in the accomplishment of your goals. Energy represents a ***measure*** of your personal capacity to produce desired outputs! What is your level of personal production and how do you measure it? Personal Productivity can and should be measured in any way meaningful to you. These measures will largely depend on your interest and dominate activities. Some measures of your personal productivity might be:

1) Income level and credit vs. potential net worth.
2) Number of books, tapes or albums you produce in
a year.
3) Number of people that you share business opportunities with in a month.
4) Number of children you put through college.
5) Number of substantive books you read or study in a
year.
6) Percentage of your income saved or invested in a
per month.
7) Number of charities you actively support.
8) Percentage of defects you correct at work.
9) Percentage of time you spend doing your daily plan.
10) Number aerobic exercise hours you get a week.

Appropriate and adapt these measures of personal productivity. Also, identify other measures that you feel are relevant and meaningful to your chosen purpose and specific desires. Learn to monitor and track these measures in a way that is easy for you. Read Stephen Covey's "Seven Basic Habits of Highly Effective People" and "Measuring, Managing and Maximizing Performance" by Will Kaydos to improve your personal productivity at work or in your business.

Anyone who has ever seen a factory has seen mechanical production of goods such as Cars, Boats, Toys and Diapers. Every machine on earth has a finite capacity; That is it can only produce a given amount of output over a given period. For instance, a sewing machine generally can only produce one dress at a time. If you want more dresses within the same period you need more sewing machines.

The principle also holds for your personal capacity to produce your purpose in meaningful, measurable terms. Appropriate and adapt these measures to your personal use. You might measure your personal capacity in the following terms:
1) Capital and personal credit vs. cost of financing
your purpose.
2) Discretionary time or effort hours available vs. time
required for your purpose.
3) Personal tools and techniques to facilitate effective,
efficient action.
4) Personal proficiency and knowledge vs. skill
required to accomplish your specific purpose.
5) Number of skilled people available and willing to   contribute to your
purpose vs. need.

Solomon's Wealth – Pharaoh's Treasures

6) Personal energy, health and stamina vs. energy
consumed and required.

Energy is transferred from one source to another in nature. For instance, all living things benefit from solar energy, when solar energy is absorbed into plants and passed throughout the food chain. Plants grow via photosynthesis and are eaten by our livestock; which are in turn eaten by you and me; by that, transferring the sun's energy into personal power which you and I can use to exercise, read, paint or otherwise work.

Consequently, energy is a prerequisite to focused action. The more energy you have the greater your endurance and perseverance. Comparatively, the more fuel you put in your car or truck, the further you can travel.

You can observe the process of transforming energy into action throughout nature. King Solomon instructs in proverbs 6:6-8 **"Go to the ant, you sluggard;** *consider her ways,* **and be** *wise***; which having no guide, overseer, or ruler provides her food in the summer, and gathers her food in the harvest."**

Interestingly, studying social insects, in particular ants and bees, has contributed tremendous insights into nature's secrets of success. Self-initiative, definite purpose and team work are but a few of these precious lessons. King Solomon, like many modern scientists and naturalist, discovered that human beings can benefit enormously by studying and applying some strategies of tiny role models.

Ants and bees are not active in the colder months or climates; therefore it is essential that they are both efficient and effective in gathering, storing and using the energy. Their energy source is primarily the foods they eat during the warmer seasons. If they fail to do this they will not survive until the next season.

Consider the farmers and agriculturists, who work the land to provide us with sustenance and energy. If they do not till the ground, plant seeds and harvest the crop at the proper time for any reason survival becomes very difficult.

It is a fact that your personal energy is directly proportional to the quantity and quality of the foods you eat. In addition to the amount of exercise and rest that you receive, decides how much energy you need. Fortunately, there are volumes of information on proper diet and exercise available in bookstore an libraries. Therefore, we shall save a few trees and defer you to them.

The main point that you need to grasp here is that to personally produce your goals and aspirations you need personal energy. Use your available resources to build and sustain your personal energy.

Needless to state, drug abuse, alcohol and sex abuse, shamelessly waste one of your most precious resources. Realize that your personal energy is one of your major bank accounts and you are the bank. When you make deposits, you increase your potential wealth; therefore when you make wise investment through Focused Action, you increase your real wealth as measured by your accomplishment.

For example, when you saw Michael Jordan eating a box of Wheaties cereal, he was depositing energy in his account. When he turned to the check out stand to cash in some game winning baskets, he has energy to spare. As a result, his team has won consecutive world basketball championships and Michael has won many personal awards.

To transform your Personal Power into achievement, you must first have the necessary amount of energy. Then you can use the A^5 formula described in the previous chapter for definite success.

Take notice therefore that Personal Power and Constancy of Focus are at the heart of the A^5 process. That is, you must follow the formula with diligence, determination and personal commitment.

However always remember, that diligence and determination begin with an intense need or definite desire, along with accurate plans for obtainment. The principles of autosuggestion, wisdom, faith and all the other principles mentioned in this book will help develop these prerequisites.

Key Points to remember

Diligence, Determination and Focused ACTION

☥ Universal Force of Habit engraves the results of every action that dominates your activities into your subconscious. This establishes patterns of behavior and thoughts necessary to satisfy the **reason or cause** of your actions.

☥ The action or behavior oriented principles are timeless causes of achievement; specifically, *diligence, determination, perseverance, persistence, relentlessness and commitment.*

☥ The Ps and Os are as follows: **Prayer, Practice, Persistence, Perseverance, Potential, Purpose, Patience, Plan, Proactivity, Prioritization, Principle, Productivity, Proficiency, Positivity, Preparation** and ***Organization, Observation, Optimization, Open mindedness, Opportunity and Question***. Use them wisely and liberally.

☥ Use the **RAPP** and T^2L^2 to construct positive habits and cause you to win your dreams from life.

☥ *Focused action* is the means by which you shall express your definite plans for causing the achievement of your purpose and desires. It makes use of Dr. Deming's world famous principle of Total Quality, **Constancy of Purpose.**

PROSPERITY and RICHES

"**Riches** and honor *are* with me: yes, durable riches   and righteousness."

-King Solomon [Pro. 8:18]

"*Peace* be within your walls, and **prosperity** within   your palaces."   -King David [Psa. 122:7]

ince the earliest civilizations of Africa and the Middle-East, men and women have sought and acquired material riches and pleasures. As mentioned in the introduction, archaeology has uncovered evidence of enormous prosperity and treasures in precious metals, elaborate dwellings and lavish clothing.

Prosperity is the condition of relative abundance and personal wealth; **Riches** are signs and tools of the condition of prosperity. This does not imply that everyone wants or need to be as prosperous as King Solomon or Andrew Carnegie. **"Remove far from me vanity and lies: give me neither poverty nor riches; Feed me with food convenient for me." [Proverbs 30:8]**

Material riches, such as money, jewelry or houses, are means to an end. That is, you use money as the *means* to buy a new boat, for your recreation or a new book, for your personal enjoyment. As a means to an end, money and riches are neither good nor evil, but may be used for either constructive or destructive purposes. For instance, the same money that bought the weapons which killed President Kennedy, Dr. King, Malcolm X and many others, should have been used to help improve the world for everyone.

What specifically causes the condition of prosperity and what prevents it? Firmly place this question in your mind, as you read this chapter and you will be better able to cause prosperity in your life. To help you begin unfolding the answer, I would like to *promote* and *advocate* three sources of information to help you understand and produce the condition of prosperity. These three sources are: **1**) The Bible, **2**) The works of Napoleon Hill; Such as *Think and Grow Rich*, **3**) Personal practices and observation.

"Your word is a lamp unto my feet, and a light unto my path." **King David[Psa. 119:105]**

Foremost is the Bible, the most wide read and distributed book ever known to humankind. The Bible is an excellent place to begin the search for the causes of personal prosperity and riches. It is a powerful guide for a variety of life skills; such as, successful spiritual and family living, commerce, science, and history.
****

However, if you have not already done so, do a little research and thinking about how to best study the bible for practical, everyday use. To help you with this I will briefly, share some principles and guidelines that you'll find useful when searching for understanding and reason in your bible.

Solomon's Wealth – Pharaoh's Treasures

I believe that the most important goals or targets of bible study are *Accuracy, Understanding and Action*. I hope to cover this topic in more detail in a later volume. Therefore, I must necessarily be brief and constrained!

The bible as we know it is a *collection* of historical and **inspirational** books written by and from the view point of the Ancient Hebrew-Israelites, including the tribes of Judah and Levi. However, there are other perspectives of this history and inspiration.

For instance, history reveals that many nations carry the story of the Great Flood in Genesis. Babylonian history particularly parallels the Hebrew accounts of the flood. Furthermore, any study (*worthy of that name*) of Ancient **Hebrew** *history* **and** *inspiration* **without in-depth study of Ancient, African Egyptian** *history* **and** *inspiration* **is doomed to error, and misunderstanding**.

Therefore, I highly recommend comparing Hebrew history to other histories of the same *region and period*, especially Egyptian, Assyrian, Babylonian and Grecian. And, I further recommend that your bible study follow a curriculum of subjects; Most notably, *Mental Science*, Applied Numerology, Natural Science, Business and Commerce, Culture, geopolitics and Religion.

Finally, serious study of any material should be supplemented by ***prayer, meditation, autosuggestion and open minded discussion***.
****

Prosperity and Riches

The Old Testament clearly reveals some main tenets of wealth building. Recall, in the books of Kings and Chronicles, that the Kings of Tyre provided other nations with *skilled* carpenters, masons, and raw materials in *exchange* for such goods as wheat and oil[2 Chron. 2:11-18].

Ezek. 28:4- "With your **wisdom** and with your **understanding** you have gotten you riches, and have gotten *gold* and *silver* into your treasures; By your great wisdom and by your **trade** have you increased your **riches**, and *your heart is lifted up because of your riches*."

Tyre and Sidon were the major trading centers of their time. Merchants bought and sold merchandise from all the others nations and cultures advanced enough to engage in commerce. Many tremendous fortunes were built through the activity of these wealthy port cities. Much like the major trading centers of our modern age, i.e. New York, Brussels, and Tokyo, Tyre helped to create and spread riches.

By applying wisdom and understanding to the business of trade and commerce; the King of Tyre *caused* his riches and prosperity to increase. *However, the seed of its destruction is in his arrogant dependence on his wealth.* Wisdom's admonishment is: "**He that *trusts* in his *riches* shall *fall*, but the *righteous* shall *flourish* like a branch.**"[Pro. 11:28]

Remember that many righteous people of the bible were rich and prosperous; yet they retained the **wealth** of good character, faith and diligence. Abraham and Lot had an abundance of cattle and sheep. "And Lot also, who went with Abraham, had flocks, and herds, and tents. And the land was not able to bear them, that they might dwell together; For their substance was great, so that could not dwell together." [Gen. 13:5, 6]

Esau and his brother Jacob also lived in prosperity. "And, Esau took his wives, and his sons, and his daughters, and all the persons of his house, and all his beast, and all his substance which he had in the land of Canaan; and went into country from the face of his brother, Jacob. For their riches were more than that they might dwell together; and the land wherein they were strangers could not bear them because of their cattle."[Gen. 36:6, 7]

Joseph, the son of Jacob-Israel, applied his wisdom and faith to resolve the Pharaoh's problems and administrate the king's business. As a result he earned the second highest job in the country as Vizier. "And Pharaoh said unto Joseph; See I have set you over all the land of Egypt."[Gen. 41:41]

King Solomon built upon his inheritance from David by shrewdly trading his *skill* and *knowledge*, materials and servants to other powerful nations and Kings. Remember his very first wife was the daughter of the powerful Pharaoh of Egypt. Furthermore, he built wealth and trade with southern Arabia and Ethiopia through his very personal relationship with the famous Queen of Sheba.

Furthermore, Joseph of Arimathaea apparently built more than material riches in trading his skills as a counselor. "When the evening was come, there came a *rich* man of Arimathaea, named Joseph, who also himself was Jesus' disciple; He went to Pilate, and begged the body of Jesus. Then Pilate commanded the body to be delivered."[Matthew 27:57,58]. Luke described- "And, behold, there was a man named Joseph, a *counselor*: and he was a good and righteous man"[Luke 23:50].

How did these biblical, historical figures **cause** prosperous conditions in their lives? This question warrants your diligent attention and prompt action. For, if you can understand and use the keys to Solomon's Wealth *you can build your own prosperity to order*.

"Wealth *gotten* by vanity shall be diminished, but he that gathers by *labor* shall increase." King Solomon [13:11]

The second major reference source for information on the causes and prevention of prosperity are the works of Dr. Napoleon Hill, particularly his landmark classics "Think and Grow Rich," and "The Law of Success." If you are among the few who have not studied and practice the principles of Dr. Hill's work; *you are rendering yourself a serious disservice*! Dr. Hill was a very diligent bible student.

Undoubtedly his depth of understanding grew considerably during the *25 years* that he researched and organzied a course on the *Science of Personal Acheivement*. In these works, Hill strongly advocates Emerson's essay on Compensation, Andrew Carnegie's secret to success and many other astounding facts and truths which harmonize with biblical principles.

Think and Grow Rich is the most distinguished self-help or success literature available, short of the Bible itself! Careful, purposeful study versus an introductory reading of this book is both fulfilling and rewarding.

That is, studying Dr. Hill's classics, lead to the related works of other intriguing authors; such as Thomas Troward, Ralph W. Emerson, Dr. William James and most recently Dr. Dennis Kimbro, co-author of *Think and Grow Rich*: **A Black Choice**.

Your understanding and application of Dr. Hill's work will greatly improve by supplementing it with related subjects and authors. So, build your PAL around such literature and tapes to enrich your personal experiences of enduring wealth.

This brings us to the third major source of information on our questions of prosperity and riches that is *personal practice* and *observation*. Yes, personal practice is essential to your understanding and assimilation of the things which attract riches.

It is very important that you diligently practice, practice, practice the teachings and techniques that you are including in your Personal Achievement Library. When you do, you are taking control of what you shall experience, versus allowing some one or some thing to decide your life's experiences for you.

Also, observe your results through any practical means available to you, and adjust your practice or plans to best complete your goals. Observe your conversations about wealth, your thoughts and beliefs, your situations and circumstances.

Undoubtedly, if you have spent your time and money with people or things which attract abundance, you have experienced prosperity. On the other hand, if you have spent your time and money with people or on things of scarcity, poverty and lack; you have experienced the things which destroy prosperity. Make conscious use the **Law of Attraction**, when you choose your acquaintances and past times.

"My fruit is better than gold, yes than fine gold; and my revenue than choice silver."
Proverbs 8:18.

Consideration of each of these three references reveals that there are primarily two major forms or categories of riches: Physical and Non-physical, tangible and intangible or material and immaterial. For instance, your new car or home is a form of physical riches, while your wisdom and faith are intangible forms of riches.

Physical riches and prosperity are all outward evidence of your effort and energy to succeed. Credit, clothes, health, houses, cars, boats, jewelry, businesses and other investments all add to your quality of life. These riches are intended to provide everything from entertainment to college education. They are tools and instruments with which men and woman seek to enjoy life.

"Behold that which I have seen"; decries Solomon "it is good and fitting for one to eat and to drink, and to enjoy the good of all his labor that he takes under the sun, all the days of his life, which God gives him; for it is his portion. Every man also to whom God has given riches and wealth, and has given him power to eat of it, and to take his portions, and rejoice in his labor; this is the gift of God."[Ecc. 5:18, 19]

Intangible riches are internal, invisible, personal and powerful. Some of your major forms of immaterial wealth are *peace of mind* and *mental health*, *character-force*, *energy*, *personal power*, specialized *skill* and *knowledge*. Intangible forms of riches are very powerful and enduring.

Therefore, as you might have known, these two major categories of riches apparently require balance or equilibrium between each other. That is you must divide your time, attention and energy wisely between enjoyment of material assets and your development, use and maintenance of immaterial wealth.

This is a very important point; do not pass over it lightly. If you have ever made the mistake of over balancing or extreme focus on either category, you already recognize the importance of equilibrium. If not, imagine or observe if you can what happens when people get narrowly focused on finding material wealth at any cost.

By the dictates universal laws of nature, they suffer proportionately in their relationships, health and other intangible forms of riches. Conversely, imagine or observe someone extremely focused on knowledge and understanding; but do not take care of practical, material matters. Some of them become derelicts of society, whether through ignorance or choice.

****

The relationship between these two forms of riches is the key to maintaining both. *Consider this point, you learned from the chapter on Thoughts and Tools. Humankind created tools with their imagination and thoughts, and used these tools to build and live their thoughts, ideals and dreams.*

Consciously use some of your **physical riches** to help you uncover and enjoy your **intangible riches**. For instance, use some of your money to buy good books, tapes and videos to help you enjoy learning and developing your character and skills. **Buy** music, poetry and art which **trigger thoughts** of **character**, **principles** and **positive action** in you. *"Buy the truth and sell it not: also* **wisdom**, *and* **instruction**, **understanding**"- wrote King Solomon [Pro. 23:23]

"Ho, every one that thirsts, come to the **waters**, and he that has **no money**; *come, buy* and eat; yes, come, buy wine and milk **without price**. *Why do you spend money for that which is not bread? And your labor for that which satisfies not? Listen* **diligently**

Solomon's Wealth – Pharaoh's Treasures

unto me, and eat *that which is good*, and let your **soul delight** itself in fatness."- wrote Isaiah 55:1, 2

And, use your inherent, unfolding spiritual and mental riches to direct your physical **conditions**. Learn to control and direct your *whole* **Attention-Awareness**, mental and physical, on your most important desires and off irrelevant distractions or fears.
****

Furthermore, use some of your money and time to maintain your general intellect. And, increase your specialized knowledge and skills in any area that you feel you really love or enjoy. By accounts of the references used in this book, including the *BIBLE* and *LAW OF SUCCESS*, you will increase in both forms of riches.

Also, you are instructed to use all of the intangible riches at your immediate disposal to increase or maintain and enjoy your material prosperity. For instance, use your wisdom, faith and energy to pursue your major purpose and definite desires. Reflect on all the principles of Solomon's Wealth.

Assimilate and apply these principles in your life, through autosuggestion. Do not be discouraged if your first attempts seem awkward or insincere. Remember everlasting persistence and an obsession to do anything definite, causes you to *accomplish the thing, that you may have the power.*

Basically whatever you do to earn your livelihood, you trade energy, time, knowledge and skill for material riches and other forms of compensations. Those with the highest quantity and quality of internal riches to trade, tend to command better prices for their "wares" than those with less. Most employers and consumers like to get at least what they pay for.

General research bears out that people with higher degrees of true education and learning, tend to have a higher average income than those who don't. I'm referring to true education, applied knowledge, not necessarily academic achievement. Remember this simple fact the next time you have to choose between *Mind Extension University* and some entertainment programs on your television set.

Adopt a positive, balanced attitude toward riches in all of its forms, so that you may enjoy the fruits of your labors. Also do not be discouraged if your equilibrium or personal emphasis is some what cyclical, seasonal or dynamic. Sometimes, you may need to be very focused on one form of riches or the other; just remember to come back to your most comfortable balance.

Your balance point should feel personal to you; because you are different, with your own taste and mind. However, remember that you must spend adequate time working, creating, producing wealth and prosperity to maintain your balance. Make certain time to learn and use sound principles that improve your life, also time to drive that new car or boat.

Intangible wealth is traded for material prosperity. How are you using your intangible assets and riches?

Solomon's Wealth – Pharaoh's Treasures

Prosperity is the condition of relative abundance and personal wealth; **Riches** are signs and tools of the condition of prosperity.

The Bible is the widest read and distributed book ever known to humankind. Your bible is an excellent place to begin the search for the causes of personal prosperity and riches. It is a powerful guide for a variety of life skills; such as, successful spiritual and family living, commerce, science, and history.

Napoleon Hill's landmark classics "Think and Grow Rich," also "Law of Success," advocates Emerson's essay on *Compensation*, Andrew Carnegie's *"secret to success"* and many other outstanding examples of characters and characteristics which cause success.

Personal experience is essential to your understanding and use of the things which attract or repel riches.

There are primarily two major forms or categories of riches: Physical and Non-physical, tangible and intangible or material and immaterial.

The **relationship** between the two major forms of riches is the *key to maintaining* both.

Prosperity and Riches

Build your personal wealth in any way that works for you and your family.

SECTION
III

"It may have been a million years ago
The Light was kindled in the Old Dark Land
With which the illumined Scrolls are all
aglow,
That Egypt gave us her mummied hand:
This was the secret of that subtle smile
Inscrutable upon the Sphinx's face,
Now told from sea to sea, from isle to isle;
The revelation of the Old Dark Race;
Theirs was the wisdom of the Bee and Bird,
Ant, Tortoise, Beaver, working human-wise;
The ancient darkness spake with Egypt's
Word;
Hers was the primal message of the skies:
The Heavens are telling nightly of her glory,
And for all time Earth echoes her great story."

                              __Gerald Massey,
                 Egypt Light of the World

Pharaoh's True Treasure

A s you've seen throughout this work, there is considerable interaction between ancient Egypt and the ancient Hebrew nation. Serious Bible students recognize this interaction from the very beginnings of the Old Testament throughout the New. This fact is important to our purposes, because it provides an avenue for us to take practical advantage of the best of both worlds.

Each of these cultures contributed considerable advice, knowledge, instruction and truth for the benefit and enlightenment of humankind. Yes, the contributions of these ancient peoples continue to brighten the path, from the old dark caves of their experiences, to the light of of our time today.

However, we do admit there is considerable argument about the historical accuracy of the Hebrew history, most of us know as the Bible. Many scholars assert that the Bible is largely metaphorical and intended to be understood in the 'spirit' of the stories rather than the exact letter of the text. Nonetheless, biblical reference to specific historical names and places give a considerable credence, at least to this author's satisfaction, of the practical value of the biblical narrative.

In contrast, there is little argument about the historical accuracy of the math, science, culture, art and philosophy of ancient Egyptian monuments and scrolls. That is to say, archaeological evidence of ancient Egypt is much more concrete and indisputable than the Hebrew history, in those terms.

Solomon's Wealth – Pharaoh's Treasures

Though many Pharaoh's exaggerated their history and bent the truth to favor their individual legacy and exploits. Nevertheless, ancient Egyptian history is supported by archaeological evidence. For instance, Pharaoh Ramses II proclaimed himself to be the greatest of all time and built many monuments to support this claim. He has some of the most magnificent monuments of the historical record.

Therefore, our purpose, in this Section, is to focus and highlight the practical value, spiritual benefit and cultural significance of the content of ancient Egyptian Thought, Counsel, Wisdom and Instruction. The next few pages will spotlight some select excerpts from important historical works to help make practical benefit of this Book.

We sincerely hope that you will follow through and appreciate the intent of the original authors of this content; starting with the original writers, monuments and the scrolls upon which they were found.

"The history of man on this planet from prehistoric times until now is a continuous whole. There is no fact, however remote, that does not have a bearing of greater or lesser importance on the destiny of the whole human race. Much has been buried, lost, forgotten but within man's consciousness is a burning desire to know as much of it as possible. Within the past four centuries this desire has increased until today there is no civilized land without a museum. In these museums are momentoes of the past which, though they might seem valueless to some, are precious to the

scientists, scholar, thinker. On excavations in Upper Egypt I noticed that every spadeful of earth was carefully sifted lest some article of the ancient past be lost, even though but a bead." __**J. A. Rogers,**
Africa's Gift To America

Pharaoh's True Treasures

THE TITLE OF PHARAOH

'Son of man, take up a lamentation for
Pharaoh King of Egypt, and say unto him,
Thou wast likened unto a young lion of the
nations.'
                              Ezekiel 27:2

"By-the-by, so far as hitherto known, the
name of 'pharaoh' is only found in Hebrew.
Some Egyptologists derive it from *par-ao*, the
great house. The present writer is of opinion
that this title of the Ra was more probably
derived from *paru* the lion than from *para* the
house. The pharaoh personated the lion, or the
lion-god, and sometimes wore the lion's tail as
the emblem of royalty. Then he was *paru* as
the lion and the *hak* as ruler. Thus the king as
lion-ruler would be the Paruhak (pharaoh)."

__Gerald Massey
Ancient Egypt Light of the World

The preceding quote is in an example of the
excellent work that, Gerald Massey,
researched and published, to help draw a more
accurate picture of ancient Egyptian culture
within its own context. It is a massive, in-
depth revelation of the true history and
philosophy of the culture and its highest

leaders. His masterpiece Ancient Egypt Light of the World is two volumes of 12 excellent Books.

I mentioned this for the benefit of historical accuracy and to affirm that the word 'Pharaoh' is used in this work simply because it's a more common reference than the actual word that the original peoples, who referred to themselves as KMT (Kemet), would have used.

That being the case, this section is to highlight the Thought and Behaviors which the Pharaohs embodied and promulgated throughout their Kingdom and Culture through Viziers(Royal Advisor), Priest and a well-organized bureaucracy. Pharaohs, were not only their kingdom's political and economic leadership, they were society's moral and ethical examples. They built deep schools of thought on wisdom, understanding and many other important principles like balance and order in ones life.

The writings in the next few pages show the extent to which Egyptian philosophy helped build one of the greatest civilizations the world has ever known.

ANCIENT WISDOM and UNDERSTANDING

The primary idea behind Egyptian philosophy was that the purpose of mankind was to live a righteous, balanced, moral existence, known to them as 'Maat', in order to attain spiritual enlightenment and fulfillment in the afterlife.

In this Author's opinion; nothing personifies this idea better than the writings of ptah-hotep. **Ptah-hotep** was vizier under Jedkare Isesi during the fifth Dynasty, c.2350 BCE. The teachings attributed to him were most likely written during the Middle Kingdom.

"The most ancient wisdom was oral; it was conveyed by word of mouth, from mouth to ear, as in the mysteries. This consisted of the magical sayings or the great words of power. Following the oral wisdom, the earliest known records of written wisdom were collections of the sayings, which were continually enlarged, as by the Egyptian Jesus, or 'the two of this name.' The Osirian *Book of the Dead* is largely a collection of sayings which were given by Ra the father in heaven to Horus the son, for him to utter as teacher of the living on earth and preacher to the manes in Amenta. The wisdom of Ptah the father was uttered by the son, who is the Word in person. The names for the son may be various in the several religious cults, but the type was one, no matter what the name. The sayings collected in some of the Hebrew books of wisdom, such as the *Book of Proverbs*, are spoken as from the father to his son. 'My son, attend to my words; incline thine ear unto my sayings. *Prov.* 4:20. 'Hear me, O my son,'[p.517] is the formula in the *Book of Ecclesiasticus*. It has now to be suggested that the mythical or divine originals of this father and son in the books of wisdom were the wise god Ptah and the youthful sage Iu, the *sayer* or *logos*, who was his manifesting word as the son. Egyptian literature as such has been almost entirely lost, but amongst the survivals lives the oldest book in the world. This is a book of wisdom, in the form of sayings, maxims, precepts, and other brief sentences, called the *Proverbs of Ptah-Hetep*, which was written in the reign of Tet-Ka-Ra or Assa, a pharaoh of the fifth dynasty, who lived 5,500 years ago. The author's name denotes that he was the worshipper of Ptah, and his collection contains the ancient wisdom of Ptah, although it is not directly ascribed to the god or to his son, the *sayer*, Iu-em-hetep. In this volume Ptah-Hetep collects the good sayings, precepts, and proverbs of the ancient wisdom; the words of those who have heard the counsels of former days and the counsels heard of the gods. He addresses the god Ptah for authority to declare these words of wisdom, speaking as from a father to his son; and in reply 'the majesty of this god says, Instruct him in the sayings of former days.'(Records of the past, 2nd Series, vol. iii,p. 17). Ptah-Hetep, then, the author who wrote a book with his own name to it 5,500 years since, assumes the position of the wise god Ptah addressing his son Iu-em-hetep, to whom the wisdom was communicated which was uttered in 'the wise sayings, dark sentences, and parables,' and collected in such books as the Sayings of Jesus, the Wisdom of Jesus, the Wisdom of Ecclesiastes, the Wisdom of Solomon, the Psalms, and the Book of the Dead. We quote a few of the sayings from ptah-hetep, which give us a sense of the intellectual height attained by the Egyptians 5,500 years ago. "

__Gerald Massey

Solomon's Wealth – Pharaoh's Treasures

Ancient Egypt Light Of The World
Vol. I Book 7, Pg., 397

Ptah-hotep was son of and vizier to King Assa of the Fifth Egpytian Dynasty. The text below was found in Thebes and can be seen today on display in the Louvre. Ptah-hotep himself, who had grown to old and experienced, wanted to pass on to his son the wisdom of his years. The book of Precepts he wrote is considered the oldest known book and is designed to teach virtue and excellence.

Horne, Charles F. *The Sacred Books and Early Literature of the East*. New York: Parke, Austin, & Lipscomb, 1917. pp. 62-78.

The Precepts of PTAH-HOTEP

Precepts of the perfect the feudal Lord Ptah-hotep, under the Majesty of the King of the South and North, Assa, living eternally forever.

The perfect, the feudal lord, Ptah-hotep, say is: O God with the two crocodiles, my lord, the progress of age changes into senility. Decay falls upon man and the decline takes the place of youth. A vexation weighs upon him every day; sight fails, the ear becomes deaf; his strength dissolves without ceasing. The mouth is silent, speech fails him; the mind decays, remembering not the day before. The whole body suffers. That which is good becomes evil; taste completely disappears. Old age makes a man altogether miserable; the nose is stopped up, breathing no more from exhaustion. Standing or sitting there is here a condition of...who will cause me to have my authority to speak, that I've made declared to him the words of those who have heard the counsels of former days? And the counsels heard of the gods, who give me authority to declare them? Calls that he be so and that evil be removed from those that are enlightened; send the double...The majesty of this god says: instruct him in the sayings of the former days. It is this which constitutes the merit of the children of the great. All that which makes the sole equal penetrates him who hears it, and that which it says produces satiety.

Beginning of the arrangement of the good sayings, spoken by the noble lord, the divine father, beloved of God, the son of the King, the firstborn of his race, the perfect and feudal lord Ptah-hotep, so as to instruct the ignorant and the knowledge of good sayings. It is profitable for him who hears them; it is lost to him who shall transgress them. He says to his son: be not arrogant because of that which you know; deal with the ignorant as with the learned; for the barriers of art are not closed, no artist being in possession of the perfection to which he should aspire. But good words are more difficult to find them the emerald, for it is by slaves that this is discovered among the rocks of the pegmatite.

Solomon's Wealth – Pharaoh's Treasures

If you find a disputant while he is hot, and if
he is superior to you in ability, lowered the
hands, bend the back; do not get into a passion
with him. As he will not let you destroy his
words, it is utterly wrong to interrupt him; that
proclaims that you are incapable of keeping
yourself calm, when you are contradicted.
If then you have to do with a disputant while
he is hot, imitate one who does not stir. You
have the advantage over him if you keep silent
when he is uttering evil words. "The better of
the two is he who is impassive," say the
bystanders and you are right in the opinion of
the great.

If you find a disputant while he is hot, do not
despise him because you are not of the same
opinion. Be that angry against him when he is
wrong; away with such a thing. He fights
against himself; require him not further to
flatter your feelings. Do not amuse yourself
with spectacle which you have before you; it
is odious, it is mean, it is the part of a
despicable soul so to do. As soon as you let
yourself be moved by your feelings, combat
this desire as a thing that is reproved by the
great.

If you have, as leader, to decide on the
conduct of a great number of men, seek the
most perfect manner of doing so that your
own conduct may be without reproach. Justice
is great, in variable, and assured; it has not
been disturbed since the age of Osiris. To
throw obstacles in the way of the laws is to
open the way before violence. Shall that
which is below gain the upperhand, if the
unjust does not attain to the place of justice?
Even he who says: I take for myself, of my

own free-will; but say not: I take by virtue of my authority. The limitations of justice are in variable; such is the instruction which every man receives from his father.

Inspire not me and with fear, else God will fight against you in the same manner. If anyone asserts that he lives by such means, God will take away the bread from his mouth; if anyone asserts that he enriches himself thereby, God says: I may take these riches to myself. If anyone asserts that he beat others, God will end by reducing him to impotence. Let no one inspire men with fear; this is the will of God. Let no one provide sustenance for them in the lap of peace; it will then be that they will freely give what has been torn from them by terror.

If you are among the persons seated at meat in the house of a greater man than yourself, take that which he gives you, bowing to the ground. Regard that which is placed before you, but point not at it; regard it not frequently; he is a blameworthy person who departs from this rule. Speak not to the great man more than he requires, for one knows not what may be displeasing to him. Speak when he invites you and your worth will be pleasing.
As for the great man who has plenty of means of existence, his conduct is as he himself wishes. He does that which pleases him; if he desires to repose, he realizes his intention. The great man stretching forth his hand does that to which other men do not attain. But as the means of existence are under the will of Ptah, one can not rebel against it.

Solomon's Wealth – Pharaoh's Treasures

If you are one of those who bring the
messages of one great man to another,
conform yourself exactly to that wherewith he
has charged you; perform for him the
commission as he has enjoined you. Beware
of altering in speaking the offensive words
which one great person addresses to another;
he who perverts the trustfulness of his way, in
order to repeat only what produces pleasure in
the words of every man, great or small, is a
detestable person.

If you are an agriculturist, gather the
crops in the field which the great Ptah has
given you, fill not your mouth in the house of
your neighbors; it is better to make oneself
dreaded by one's deeds. As for him who,
master of his own way of acting, being all-
powerful, seizes the goods of others like a
crocodile in the midst even of watchment, his
children are an object of malediction, of scorn,
and of hatred on account of it, while his father
is grievously distressed, and as for the mother
who has borne him, happy is another rather
than herself. But a man becomes a god when
he is chief of a tribe which has confidence in
following him.

If you abase yourself in obeying a
superior, your conduct is entirely good before
Ptah. Knowing who you ought to obey and
who you ought to command, do not lift up
your heart against him. As you know that in
him is authority, be respectful toward him as
belonging to him. Wealth comes only at Ptah's
own good-will, and his caprice only is the
law; as for him who ... Ptah, who has created
his superiority, turns himself from him and he

is overthrown.

Be active during the time of your existence, doing more than is commanded. Do not spoil the time of your activity; he is a blameworthy person who makes a bad use of his moments. Do not lose the daily opportunity of increasing that which your house possesses. Activity produces riches, and riches do not endure when it slackens.

If you are a wise man, bring up a son who shall be pleasing to Ptah. If he conforms his conduct to your way and occupies himself with your affairs as is right, do to him all the good you can; he is your son, a person attached to you whom your own self has begotten. Separate not your heart from him.... But if he conducts himself ill and transgresses your wish, if he rejects all counsel, if his mouth goes according to the evil word, strike him on the mouth in return. Give orders without hesitation to those who do wrong, to him whose temper is turbulent; and he will not deviate from the straight path, and there will be no obstacle to interrupt the way.

If you are employed in the larit, stand or sit rather than walk about. Lay down rules for yourself from the first: not to absent yourself even when weariness overtakes you. Keep an eye on him who enters announcing that what he asks is secret; what is entrusted to you is above appreciation, and all contrary argument is a matter to be rejected. He is a god who penetrates into a place where no relaxation of the rules is made for the privileged.

Solomon's Wealth – Pharaoh's Treasures

If you are with people who display for you an extreme affection, saying: "Aspiration of my heart, aspiration of my heart, where there is no remedy! That which is said in your heart, let it be realized by springing up spontaneously. Sovereign master, I give myself to your opinion. Your name is approved without speaking. Your body is full of vigor; your face is above your neighbors." If then you are accustomed to this excess of flattery, and there be an obstacle to you in your desires, then your impulse is to obey your passion. But he who . . . according to his caprice, his soul is . . ., his body is . . . While the man who is master of his soul is superior to those whom Ptah has loaded with his gifts; the man who obeys his passion is under the power of his wife.

Declare your line of conduct without reticence; give your opinion in the council of your lord; while there are people who turn back upon their own words when they speak, so as not to offend him who has put forward a statement, and answer not in this fashion: "He is the great man who will recognize the error of another; and when he shall raise his voice to oppose the other about it he will keep silence after what I have said."

If you are a leader, setting forward your plans according to that which you decide, perform perfect actions which posterity may remember, without letting the words prevail with you which multiply flattery, which excite pride and produce vanity.

If you are a leader of peace, listen to the discourse of the petitioner. Be not abrupt with him; that would trouble him. Say not to him: "You have already recounted this." Indulgence will encourage him to accomplish the object of his coming. As for being abrupt with the complainant because he described what passed when the injury was done, instead of complaining of the injury itself let it not be! The way to obtain a clear explanation is to listen with kindness.

If you desire to excite respect within the house you enter, for example the house of a superior, a friend, or any person of consideration, in short everywhere where you enter, keep yourself from making advances to a woman, for there is nothing good in so doing. There is no prudence in taking part in it, and thousands of men destroy themselves in order to enjoy a moment, brief as a dream, while they gain death, so as to know it. It is a villainous intention, that of a man who thus excites himself; if he goes on to carry it out, his mind abandons him. For as for him who is without repugnance for such an act, there is no good sense at all in him.

If you desire that your conduct should be good and preserved from all evil, keep yourself from every attack of bad humor. It is a fatal malady which leads to discord, and there is no longer any existence for him who gives way to it. For it introduces discord between fathers and mothers, as well as between brothers and sisters; it causes the wife and the husband to hate each other; it contains all kinds of wickedness, it embodies all kinds of wrong. When a man has established his just equilibrium and walks in this path, there

where he makes his dwelling, there is no room
for bad humor.

Be not of an irritable temper as regards that
which happens beside you; grumble not over
your own affairs. Be not of an irritable temper
in regard to your neighbors; better is a
compliment to that which displeases than
rudeness. It is wrong to get into a passion with
one's neighbors, to be no longer master of
one's words. When there is only a little
irritation, one creates for oneself an affliction
for the time when one will again be cool.

If you are wise, look after your house; love
your wife without alloy. Fill her stomach,
clothe her back; these are the cares to be
bestowed on her person. Caress her, fulfil her
desires during the time of her existence; it is a
kindness which does honor to its possessor.
Be not brutal; tact will influence her better
than violence; her . . . behold to what she
aspires, at what she aims, what she regards. It
is that which fixes her in your house; if you
repel her, it is an abyss. Open your arms for
her respond to her arms; call her, display to
her your love.
Treat your dependents well, in so far as it
belongs to you to do so; and it belongs to
those whom Ptah has favored. If any one fails
in treating his dependents well it is said: "He
is a person . . ." As we do not know the events
which may happen tomorrow, he is a wise
person by whom one is well treated. When
there comes the necessity of showing zeal, it
will then be the dependents themselves who
say: "Come on, come on," if good treatment
has not quitted the place; if it has quitted it,

the dependents are defaulters.

Do not repeat any extravagance of language;
do not listen to it; it is a thing which has
escaped from a hasty mouth. If it is repeated,
look, without hearing it, toward the earth; say
nothing in regard to it. Cause him who speaks
to you to know what is just, even him who
provokes to injustice; cause that which is just
to be done, cause it to triumph. As for that
which is hateful according to the law,
condemn it by unveiling it.

If you are a wise man, sitting in the council of
your lord, direct your thought toward that
which is wise. Be silent rather than scatter
your words. When you speak, know that
which can be brought against you. To speak in
the council is an art, and speech is criticized
more than any other labor; it is contradiction
which puts it to the proof.

If you are powerful, respect knowledge and
calmness of language. Command only to
direct; to be absolute is to run into evil. Let
not your heart be haughty, neither let it be
mean. Do not let your orders remain unsaid
and cause your answers to penetrate; but
speak without heat, assume a serious
countenance. As for the vivacity of an ardent
heart, temper it; the gentle man penetrates all
obstacles. He who agitates himself all the day
long has not a good moment; and he who
amuses himself all the day long keeps not his
fortune. Aim at fulness like pilots; once one is
seated another works, and seeks to obey one's
orders.

Solomon's Wealth – Pharaoh's Treasures

Disturb not a great man; weaken not the attention of him who is occupied. His care is to embrace his task, and he strips his person through the love which he puts into it. That transports men to Ptah, even the love for the work which they accomplish. Compose then your face even in trouble, that peace may be with you, when agitation is with . . .These are the people who succeed in what they desire.

Teach others to render homage to a great man. If you gather the crop for him among men, cause it to return fully to its owner, at whose hands is your subsistence. But the gift of affection is worth more than the provisions with which your back is covered. For that which the great man receives from you will enable your house to live, without speaking of the maintenance you enjoy, which you desire to preserve; it is thereby that he extends a beneficent hand, and that in your home good things are added to good things. Let your love pass into the heart of those who love you; cause those about you to be loving and obedient.

If you are a son of the guardians deputed to watch over the public tranquillity, execute your commission without knowing its meaning, and speak with firmness. Substitute not for that which the instructor has said what you believe to be his intention; the great use words as it suits them. Your part is to transmit rather than to comment upon.

If you are annoyed at a thing, if you are tormented by someone who is acting within his right, get out of his sight, and remember him no more when he has ceased to address you.

If you have become great after having been little, if you have become rich after having been poor, when you are at the head of the city, know how not to take advantage of the fact that you have reached the first rank, harden not your heart because of your elevation; you are become only the administrator, the prefect, of the provisions which belong to Ptah. Put not behind you the neighbor who is like you; be unto him as a companion.

Bend your back before your superior. You are attached to the palace of the king; your house is established in its fortune, and your profits are as is fitting. Yet a man is annoyed at having an authority above himself, and passes the period of life in being vexed thereat. Although that hurts not your . . . Do not plunder the house of your neighbors, seize not by force the goods which are beside you. Exclaim not then against that which you hear, and do not feel humiliated. It is necessary to reflect when one is hindered by it that the pressure of authority is felt also by one's neighbor.

Do not make . . . you know that there are obstacles to the water which comes to its hinder part, and that there is no trickling of that which is in its bosom. Let it not . . . after having corrupted his heart.

If you aim at polished manners, call not him whom you accost. Converse with him especially in such a way as not to annoy him. Enter on a discussion with him only after having left him time to saturate his mind with

the subject of the conversation. If he lets his
ignorance display itself, and if he gives you all
opportunity to disgrace him, treat him with
courtesy rather; proceed not to drive him into
a corner; do not . . . the word to him; answer
not in a crushing manner; crush him not;
worry him not; in order that in his turn he may
not return to the subject, but depart to the
profit of your conversation.

Let your countenance be cheerful during
the time of your existence. When we see one
departing from the storehouse who has
entered in order to bring his share of
provision, with his face contracted, it shows
that his stomach is empty and that authority is
offensive to him. Let not that happen to you; it
is . . .

Know those who are faithful to you when you
are in low estate. Your merit then is worth
more than those who did you honor. His . . .,
behold that which a man possesses
completely. That is of more importance than
his high rank; for this is a matter which passes
from one to another. The merit of one's son is
advantageous to the father, and that which he
really is, is worth more than the remembrance
of his father's rank.

Distinguish the superintendent who directs
from the workman, for manual labor is little
elevated; the inaction of the hands is
honorable. If a man is not in the evil way, that
which places him there is the want of
subordination to authority.

If you take a wife, do not . . . Let her be more
contented than any of her fellow-citizens. She

will be attached to you doubly, if her chain is
pleasant. Do not repel her; grant that which
pleases her; it is to her contentment that she
appreciates your direction.

If you hear those things which I have said
to you, your wisdom will be fully advanced.
Although they are the means which are
suitable for arriving at the maat, and it is that
which makes them precious, their memory
would recede from the mouth of men. But
thanks to the beauty of their arrangement in
rhythm all their words will now be carried
without alteration over this earth eternally.
That will create a canvass to be embellished,
whereof the great will speak, in order to
instruct men in its sayings. After having
listened to them the pupil will become a
master, even he who shall have properly
listened to the sayings because he shall have
heard them. Let him win success by placing
himself in the first rank; that is for him a
position perfect and durable, and he has
nothing further to desire forever. By
knowledge his path is assured, and he is made
happy by it on the earth. The wise man is
satiated by knowledge; he is a great man
through his own merits. His tongue is in
accord with his mind; just are his lips when he
speaks, his eyes when he gazes, his ears when
he hears. The advantage of his son is to do
that which is just without deceiving himself.
To attend therefore profits the son of him who
has attended. To attend is the result of the fact
that one has attended. A teachable auditor is
formed, because I have attended. Good when
he has attended, good when he speaks, he who
has attended has profited, and it is profitable
to attend to him who has attended. To attend

is worth more than anything else, for it
produces love, the good thing that is twice
good. The son who accepts the instruction of
his father will grow old on that account. What
Ptah loves is that one should attend; if one
attends not, it is abhorrent to Ptah. The heart
makes itself its own master when it attends
and when it does not attend; but if it attends,
then his heart is a beneficent master to a man.
In attending to instruction, a man loves what
he attends to, and to do that which is
prescribed is pleasant. When a son attends to
his father, it is a twofold joy for both; when
wise things are prescribed to him, the son is
gentle toward his master. Attending to him
who has attended when such things have been
prescribed to him, he engraves upon his heart
that which is approved by his father; and the
recollection of it is preserved in the mouth of
the living who exist upon this earth.

When a son receives the instruction of his
father there is no error in all his plans. Train
your son to be a teachable man whose wisdom
is agreeable to the great. Let him direct his
mouth according to that which has been said
to him; in the docility of a son is discovered
his wisdom. His conduct is perfect while error
carries away the unteachable. Tomorrow
knowledge will support him, while the
ignorant will be destroyed.

As for the man without experience who listens
not, he effects nothing whatsoever. He sees
knowledge in ignorance, profit in loss; he
commits all kinds of error, always accordingly
choosing the contrary of what is praiseworthy.
He lives on that which is mortal, in this
fashion. His food is evil words, whereat he is

filled with astonishment. That which the great
know to be mortal he lives upon every day,
flying from that which would be profitable to
him, because of the multitude of errors which
present themselves before him every day.

A son who attends is like a follower of Horus;
he is happy after having attended. He becomes
great, he arrives at dignity, he gives the same
lesson to his children. Let none innovate upon
the precepts of his father; let the same
precepts form his lessons to his children.
"Verily," will his children say to him, "to
accomplish what you say works marvels."
Cause therefore that to flourish which is just,
in order to nourish your children with it. If the
teachers allow themselves to be led toward
evil principles, verily the people who
understand them not will speak accordingly,
and that being said to those who are docile
they will act accordingly. Then all the world
considers them as masters and they inspire
confidence in the public; but their glory
endures not so long as would please them.
Take not away then a word from the ancient
teaching, and add not one; put not one thing in
place of another; beware of uncovering the
rebellious ideas which arise in you; but teach
according to the words of the wise. Attend if
you wish to dwell in the mouth of those who
shall attend to your words, when you have
entered upon the office of master, that your
words may be upon our lips . . . and that there
may be a chair from which to deliver your
arguments.

Let your thoughts be abundant, but let your
mouth be under restraint, and you shall argue
with the great. Put yourself in unison with the

ways of your master; cause him to say: "He is my son," so that those who shall hear it shall say "Praise be to her who has borne him to him!" Apply yourself while you speak; speak only of perfect things; and let the great who shall hear you say: "Twice good is that which issues from his mouth!"

Do that which your master bids you. Twice good is the precept of his father, from whom he has issued, from his flesh. What he tells us, let it be fixed in our heart; to satisfy him greatly let us do for him more than he has prescribed. Verily a good son is one of the gifts of Ptah, a son who does even better than he has been told to do. For his master he does what is satisfactory, putting himself with all his heart on the part of right.

So I shall bring it about that your body shall be healthful, that the Pharaoh shall be satisfied with you in all circumstances and that you shall obtain years of life without default.

It has caused me on earth to obtain one hundred and ten years of life, along with the gift of the favor of the Pharaoh among the first of those whom their works have ennobled, satisfying the Pharaoh in a place of dignity. It is finished, from its beginning to its end, according to that which is found in writing.

In Summary,

the principles and habits described in **Section II and Section III** are your keys to pragmatic use of the enormous powers described in **Section I**. Universal principles and practices of achievement are the Keys to your marvelous natural birth rights. Many different characters, throughout recorded history, confirm the authenticity of modern self-improvement technologies and techniques.

You have an inalienable right to recognize and associate key foundation principles of your bible with certain fields of modern science. Commit today to use the precepts and practices of the science of personal achievement to access the splendid power of your own *Mind-Body* in harmony with the minds of others, *Time* and *Habit Force*.

Act immediately on the impulse to uncover your chosen purpose and major desire in life. Diligently work to submit this major purpose and desire to your *Automatic-Mind* through the principles of prayer, visualization and autosuggestion.

I have outlined and promoted to you the works of some of history's most profound instructions and guidance. The thoughts, characteristics, teachings and habits which *causes* achievement, either great or small, beckons you to your **destiny**.

You have learned from your Bible and other classics like "The Law of Success" that you are designed to share the same behavior and thoughts which caused King Solomon's and Andrew Carnegie's success. Let this light shine through your actions more than your words. Use thoughts and behavior as personal ambassadors of your sincere, genuine efforts to improve.

Anticipate the period when your initial excitement or enthusiasms stabilizes to a more permanent level. **This is the crucial period in which many people fail to follow through on their plans and purpose.** You must exercise faith, diligence and determination to employ universal natural forces to your achievement efforts.

Plan to reread this section again, after you have read the entire book. Adopt and adapt Benjamin Franklin's approach to building these principles into your character. That is, plan to understand and assimilate one set of principles at a time, until you have succeeded in building your success habits and reflexes to order.

My personal hope and **challenge** for you *yes YOU*, is that you **teach** a minimum of three people in your immediate life to learn and use the principles of this section. These three people should be yourself and one person from within your family, another outside your immediate family. Teach each other and support one another through the tough spots.

Best wishes, and may your efforts be blessed

SECTION IV

*"Your **name**, O Lord, endures forever, and your **memorial**, O Lord, throughout all generations."*

King David [Psa. 135:13]

o all of the Poets, Balladeers, Lovers and Artist; To the Teachers, Seekers, Philosophers and "Creatures" of Nature, this section is yours. To those who see with the Mind, better than with eyes and feel with the Heart, much better than with hands.

There are inevitably truths of life which transcend practical explaination. The true beauty of Universal Forces and Power can be felt better than it can seen or heard. Music, Lyrics, Poetry, and Art has declared the emotional impact of natural *flowing water*, *stary nights* and other splendid wonders of nature, upon the **heart** and at least six of the **senses** of humankind since antiquity. "The heavens declare the glory of God, and the firmament shows his handiwork." [Psalms 19:1]

Emotion is the energy which drives achievement. And, Love and Fear are two of the most powerful emotions known. Attune your heart and watch with your mind the combination of these emotions as you read such works as Psalm 119, which describes King David's experience with the **Infinite** Power and Intelligence of **Primary First-Life,**
the Almighty,
the All Beautiful,
the ALL in All,
the Living-GOD.

Heaven or Hell

In a land of Visions and Rhythms,
far beneath the Night,
where sleep liberates daydreams for
Mystical delights.
Songs carry on new rhythms,
of Magnets and Miracles alike.

I heard it said if lyrics are read
in this place in the head,
a new day is sure to dawn.

"Awake me now," I heard one yell
"For this land can be Heaven and it can be
Hell!"

Then a familiar voice cried out,
Mastery is your Right;
but you must choose well.

For then I can become fully *__Awake__* and finally
cease to wait for I **AM I**. . .
Master in your Kingdom of Influence,
Prudent in your matters of Prudence,
Wise to meet your needs,
Faithful to complete the Holy deeds of your
design. For **I AM I**.
-Jahbril

A Gift of the Wind

As the East Wind came to
blow on the flames,
so also to stimulate your thought.

With gems in hand
and jewels so grand
how priceless is that which it brought?

It is finer than Gold
and ever so bold;
It is the principal thing that is taught.

It is the Pearl of Life,
the Diamond of Love.
It is the Brilliance of Light,
the Flight of a Dove.

It is far finer than Wine,
it's the truth in the line
"there is no time like
the beautiful and ever

Present . . .

The *Future* of the
MOMENT

After the "DREAM"
and beyond "ANY MEANS"
Where does your future lie?

Is he in school or
out by the pool
playing the fool by and by?
Is she standing on her feet;
or lying in streets at the hands of a nasty high?

Where is your Martin, your Malcolm, your
Marcus;
Where is your Mary, your Martha, your
Maybelle?
Are they in living color?
or was it all just a fable?

How many Martins have been
shot in the street?
How many Marys have been
killed in their sleep?

They're dying in the arms
of violence and crack.
Shall they fall evenmore
before we find our way back.

Back to the Love of an unselfish act;
back to the Light of a world before Crack.
Back to the *ONE* where nothing is slack;
**let us each send to our Prodigals and tell
them that!**

Undergrowth

While walking in a strange Forest one day, I
observed the undergrowth in a rather
thoughtful way.

This is what I saw as I was
walking by and by. . .

A beautiful Eagle who would not try,
loaded with feathers and he would not fly!

"Your wings are as beautiful as the
mountain sky,
tell me my friend why won't fly?"

Then I saw a Rose bud who neglected to
grow, planted in fertile ground and she would
not grow! The ground was so rich yet she
would not show.

"O' tell me Rose, what do you say to the
Rain and the Sun who feed you each day,
or the Wind and the Soil ,
who sweated and fretted for you in great
Toil?"

Alas, I saw dried bones by a pool,
covered in dust, the folly of fools.
This was the *Mind* that refused to know,
at an Oasis of Knowledge and yet would not
know.
"Teach me O' Mind
that refuses to know,
Show me sweet Rose
that refuses to grow,
Tell me O' Eagle that refuses to fly.
Where did it go, when did you die?"   -Jahbril

GRACE UNDER DESIGN

GRACE is the splendor of a giant Tree,
gently swaying in the mountain breeze,
deeply rooted and yet so free.
Free to the eyes of you and me,
to teach our hearts to hear and see.

"Meditate on my demonstration,"
said he "model my natural mode.
If you anchor your roots in the *SOUL* of the
soil,
spread your branches to the *LIGHT*;
then you shall see *BEAUTY* untold,
the Grace of your *DESIGN* unfold."

My Body's love is physical delight,
but Mind is the Master Sense.
My Soul craves Spiritual flight,
ONE is *the beautiful Present*.
Spirit is my Soul in flight,
Mind is the Master Me,
Physique completes this divine design,
this can you see?

So, in the center of the depths of *SOUL*,
in inner heights *SPIRIT* moves; To give
Living Love and Life,
That hearts may be soothed.

Cease and release me O' ignorance,
abandon me arrogant ways.
Flee from me vanity and vex,
sin has end in evil days.

O' run to me and run with to me,
cry to me and fly with me;
Wisdom and Grace are life you see, Faith is
the *HOLY ONE*.   -Jahbril

Self-Control

I am moved by a mystery,
a secret of my Soul.

I am not certain of the meaning
or the hope, which is of old.

Rescue me O Understanding,
Wisdom and righteous Fear;
for to a deep hole, I am very near.

For I know not the cause
of this wonder,
that I ponder in my head.

With eyes as deep as passion
and lips as full of life,
yet also full of strife.

So the pleasure is unknown
to me, guarded by a sea from me.

My urge is to hunt this secret,
to capture this mystery.
Yet it is my delight to love
the ancient teachings, and yield to tranquility.

For though your heart is like flower
and my passion like a bee;
I'll take my fill of light, not honey
to live and learn, not toss and turn
from passionate stupidity.

-Jahbril

Songs of Spring

How lovely is your voice my dove,
how beautiful are your songs.
May I have your hand in marriage,
for I can not wait too long.

O give me of Wisdom to wife,
and Understanding as my lover,
Courage and Respect for Life,
and Prudence as my brother.

For ignorance I can't endure.
So add to me Wisdom as a wife
and my life she will insure.

Keep foolish pleasure and vain conceit,
for these defeat foolish souls.
Give my heart to Understanding,
let me be her concubine.
Give my Soul to Diligence and Faith,
as my real Valentine.

May Instruction be our wedding gift,
Peace and Joy to lift the burdened Soul.
For then I shall endure this world's
suffering and toil.

I thank you LORD for the Light of \
your anointed, ONE gave for us his life.

You lead them all from Wisdom to Faith,
to lead us all from corruption to Grace.

-Jahbril

Brothers Of Life

You are there in my beginning,
in the memories of my mind.

I remember your smiles and
grinning,
from pages of youthful times.
O how good it was to see your smile
and laughter for you are unlike any
other.

Your loving, playful therapy was the
real medicine for your brother.

If love has expression, yours for
mine,
mine for yours is a song Divine.

You are my brother in times of
trouble and deep despair,
You are my brother when life is
cruel and terribly unfair.

You are even my brother when I am
most unbrotherly, for this I love you
very deep.

So when your life is full of troubles,
my soul is to weep.
O, if I could but solve all our ills,
with
tender care and strength of Will.

Let all the world remember and feel
this truth; **Life** is for the *living*,
so is **Wealth** is for the *giving*;
Love is to *express*,
Trouble is to impress the *wise* of
Heart.

*"Who can find a virtuous woman? For her price is far above rubies. The heart of her husband does safely trust in her, so that he shall have no need of spoil She will do him good, and not evil, all the days of her life. She seeks wool, and flax, and works willingly with her hands. She is like the merchants' ship; she brings her food from afar. She rises also while it is yet night, and gives food to her household, and a portion to her maidens. She considers a field, and buys it; with the fruit of her hands she plants a vineyard. She girdes her loins with strength and strengthens her arms. She percieves that her merchandise is good; her lamp goes not out by night. She lays her hands to the spindle, and her hands the distaff. She stretches out her hands to the poor; yes, she reaches forth her hands to the needy. She is not afraid of the snow for her household; for all her household are clothed with scarlet. She makes herself coverings of tapestry; her clothing is silk and purple. Her husband is known in the gates, when he sits among the elders of the land. She makes fine linen, and sells it, and delivers girdles unto the merchant. Strength and honor are her clothing, and she shall rejoice in time to come. She opens her mouth with **wisdom**, and in her tongue is the law of kindness. She looks well to the ways of her household, and eat not the bread of idleness. Her children rise up, and call her blessed; her husband also, and the praise her. Many daughters have done virtuously, but you excell them all. **Favor is deceitful, and beauty is vain, but a woman who fears the Lord, she shall be praised.** Give her of the fruit of her hands, and let her own works praise her in the gates."*
-King Lemuel[Pro. 31:10..26-3]

To the Inner Woman

Lovely and Pure my Flower,
is the fragrance of your thoughts;
Wonderful and secure are they
when to my Heart's Mind they are brought.

Bold and Beautiful I say are you
when in your satin sleep;
for your Heart is so full of gold,
your dreams must be honey sweet.

I do adore and desire you;
My hope is to inspire you
and love you evermore.
Who are you,
O' who are you and
what are you sent to do?

Are you come on the wings of Wisdom
to calm the storms of Time?
Are you come of some great accord
to stimulate my wearied Mind?
Perhaps you were hidden in my ribs,
to show me great truths sublime?

In the "Songs of Spring"
my Soul did sing
until the heights of summer;
so again I pray that I hear you say
"I've come to share with you my highest
honor."

-Jahbril

Wisdom of Faith

O Wisdom, if you would be water,
I shall dive deeply in you,
to find the hidden keys to your devotion.

Wisdom of the ages, if you should be strong drink,
I shall soon drown in your intoxication.

Love do not fail me, Desire do not leave me, O
soul she is your life she is your life O soul, she is
your life.

O Faith in God, if you will be my snare,
I shall run to you, that I might
not escape for your prison is his Kingdom.

Faith in the Ancient of Days, if you would be my
blood, I shall cherish you as the life of my life,
that you may flow forever as the spirit of my
veins, the hope of my freedom.

Passion do not fail me, for I need
her.
Hope do not leave me; I plead
for her.
O soul she is your life,
she is your life O soul, she is your life.

You Wisdom of Faith, you Faith of Wisdom are
the beauty most; yet like a ghost
you can not be seen by them the will not see.

O daughter of Wisdom, you daughter of Faith,
your beauty should shine in my Soul and my
Mind, your love to wife is the hope of my life.

Your bosom and thighs are the desire of my eyes
that I may be yours forever, in my Heart's Mind.
-Jahbril

"Behold, how good and how pleasant it is for brethren to dwell together in **_UNITY_**! It is like the precious ointment upon the head, that ran down upon the beard, even Aaron's
    beard; that went down to the skirts of his garments, Like the dew of Hermon, and like the dew that descended upon the mountains of Zion; for there the Lord commanded the blessing, even life for evermore."
King David[Psa.133:1-3]

"I hate vain thoughts, but your *law do I love*. You are my hiding place and shield; *I **hope** in your word*. Depart from me you evildoers; for I will *keep* the commandments of my God. Uphold me according to your word that, I may live; and l*et me not be ashamed of **hope***. Hold you me up, and I shall be safe; and I will have respect unto your statues *continually*. You have trodden down all those who err from your statues; for their deceit is falsehood. You put away all the wicked of the earth like dross; therefore, I love your testimonies. My flesh trembles for *fear of you*, and I am *afraid* of your judgements."
King David[Psa. 119:113-120]

*"Bow down your ear, and **hear** the words of the wise, and **apply** your **heart** unto my knowledge. For it is a **pleasant** thing if **you keep them within you**; they shall be fitted in your lips. That your **trust** may be in the **Lord**, I have made known to **you** this day, even to **YOU**. Have not I written to **you** excellent things in **counsels** and **knowledge**. That I might make **you** know the certainty of the words of **truth**, that **you** might answer the words of truth to those who send unto **you**?"*
-King Solomon[Pro. 22:17-21]

*The Preacher sought to find out acceptable words: and that which was **written was upright, even words of truth.** The words of the wise are like goads, and like nails fastened by the master of assemblies, which are given by one sheperd. And further, by these my son, be admonished: of making many books there is no end; and much study is a weariness of the flesh. Let us hear the conclusion of the whole matter: **Fear GOD, and keep his commandments; for this is the whole duty of man.** For God shall bring every work into judgment, with every secret thing, whether it be good, or whether it be evil.*

-King Solomon[Ecc. 12:10-14]

Bibliography

I recommend that you include all of this books for your **PAL**

Ackerman, D. Dr(1990) *A Natural History of the Senses*,
New York:Vintage Books

Albrecht, K. Dr(1980) *Brain Power*, New Jersey:Prentice-Hall

Autry, J.A(1991) *Love & Profit,* New York:Morrow Company

Bullinger, E.W.(1987) *NUMBER IN SCRIPTURE*, Michigan: Kregel Publications

Casson, L.(1965) Great Ages of Man-*ANCIENT EGYPT*,
New York:TIME-LIFE Books

Coue', Emile(1923) *How to Practtice Suggestion and   Autosuggestion*, NM:Sun Publishing Company

Covey, S. Dr(1989) *The Seven Basic Habits of Highly Effective People*, New York:Simon & Schuster

Covey, S. Dr(1990) *Principle Centered Leadership*,
NewYork:Summit Books

Cox, Murray. "Forum", OMNI:*The Search for GOD*, August
1991, New York:Omni Magazine

Dumont, Theron Q. *The Master Mind*,
Chicago:Advanced   Thought Publishing
Co.

Edman, Irwin(1926) *Emerson's Essays*, New
York:Thomas Y.Crowell Company

El-Amin M.(1988) *FreeMasonry, Ancient
Egypt and the Islamic Destiny*, New
York:New Mind Productions

Gibran, K.(1989) *The PROPHET*, New
York:Afred Knopf

Howard, V(1975) *The Power of your
SuperMind*, New Jersey: Prentice-Hall

Hill, N. Dr (1979) *THE LAW OF SUCCESS*,
New Jersey:
Wehman Bros., INC.

Hill, N. Dr.(1988) *Think & Grow Rich
Action Pack*, New York: Penguin Books
USA INC.

Hill, N. Dr.(1983) *The PMA Science of
Success Course*, South Carolina: The
Napoleon Hill Foundation

Horne, Charles F.; Ph.D(1917) *The Sacred
Books And Early Literature of The East*,
Parke, Austin and Lipscomb, Inc. New York,
London

John-Roger and McWilliams P.(1991) *DO IT!
Lets Get off Our Buts*, Los Angeles:Prelude
Press

John-Roger and McWilliams P.(1992) *Wealth 101*, Los
Angeles:Prelude Press

Karenga, M. Dr(1989) *Selections from THE HUSIA*,
Los Angeles:Univ. Sankore Press

Kimbro, D. Dr. and Hill, N. Dr.(1991) *Think and Grow Rich: A Black Choice*, New York: Fawcett Columbine

Lahey, B.(1981) *Psychology*, an introduction, Iowa:WCB
Company

Legrand J.(1989) *Chronicle of the World*, Ecam Publications
distributed in the U.S. New York:Prentice-Hall

Massey, Gerald(1907)*Acient Egypt The Light Of The World,* A Work of Reclamation and Restitution,London: T. Fisher Unwin, Adelphi Terrace

Michaud, E. and Wild, R.(1991) *Boost your BRAIN POWER*, Pennsylvania:Rodale Press

Monroe, M. Dr(1991) *Understanding your Potential*,
Pennslyvania: Destiny Image Publishers

Murphy, C.B.(1989) *Dictionary of Biblical Literacy*,
Nashville:Nelson Publishers

Murphy, J. Dr(1963) *The Power of Your Subconscious Mind*,

New Jersey:Prentice-Hall

Robbins, A.(1991) *Awaken the Giant Within*, New York: Summit Books

Restak, R.M. Dr(1988) *The MIND,* New York:Bantam Books

Rogers, J.A.(1961) *AFRICA'S GIFT TO AMERICA*, St. Petersburg, FL:Helga M. Rogers

Thurman, Howard Dr.(1984) *For The INWARD JOURNEY*, Orlando, FL: Harcourt Brace Jovanovich

Troward, T.(1913) *BIBLE MYSTERY and BIBLE MEANING*, New York:G.P. Putnam's Sons

Troward, T.(1909) *The EDINBURGH LECTURES on Mental Science* , New York:G.P. Putnam's Sons

Troward, T.(1915) *The CREATIVE PROCESS in the Individual*, New York:Dodd, Mead & Company

Troward, T.(1921) *The HIDDEN POWER and other Papers upon Mental Science*, NM: Sun Publishing Co., 1993

Walton, M(1986) *The Deming Management Method*, New York:Perigee Books

Whiston, W. translator(1987) *The Works of Josephus* complete and unabridged, Massachusetts:Hendrickson Publishers

www.ingramcontent.com/pod-product-compliance
Lightning Source LLC
Chambersburg PA
CBHW061821040426
42447CB00012B/2756

* 9 780615 678382 *